Islam, Culture and Wome

An examination of the place of religion, especially Islam, in political and cultural life took on a special urgency after the events of 9/11. The essays in this volume concentrate on the way that Islam impacts on the everyday lives of people who reside in societies where Islam plays a large part. The relationship between Islam and women has always been seen as problematic, and by highlighting women's negotiations with this religion, this volume seeks to understand the many and various strategies and connections that are made, and their political and cultural ramifications.

By keeping an Asian focus, the authors also seek to understand the wide panorama that Islamic societies inhabit, and the manifold political and cultural expressions that ensue from this. The effort is not only to break the image of a monolithic structure and set of beliefs, but also to highlight on-the-ground negotiations, and the ways that women in particular find spaces within Islamic structures and discourses.

This book was originally published as a special issue of *Inter-Asia Cultural Studies.*

Firdous Azim is Professor of English and Chairperson of the Department of English and Humanities at BRAC University in Bangladesh. She is a member of Naripokkho, a woman's activist organization based in Bangladesh. She is a member of the editorial collective of IACS. Her research interests and writings include post-colonial and feminist literary analysis and issues pertaining to feminist activism. She is the author of *The Colonial Rise of the Novel* (1993).

Islam, Culture and Women in Asia

Complex Terrains

Edited by
Firdous Azim

Routledge
Taylor & Francis Group
LONDON AND NEW YORK

First published in paperback 2024

First published 2013
by Routledge
4 Park Square, Milton Park, Abingdon, Oxon OX14 4RN

and by Routledge
605 Third Avenue, New York, NY 10158

Routledge is an imprint of the Taylor & Francis Group, an informa business

This book is a reproduction of *Inter-Asia Cultural Studies*, volume 12, issue 2. The Publisher requests to those authors who may be citing this book to state, also, the bibliographical details of the special issue on which the book was based.

Publisher's Note

The publisher would like to make readers aware that the chapters in this book may be referred to as articles as they are identical to the articles published in the special issue. The publisher accepts responsibility for any inconsistencies that may have arisen in the course of preparing this volume for print.

British Library Cataloguing in Publication Data
A catalogue record for this book is available from the British Library

ISBN: 978-0-415-52826-9 (hbk)
ISBN: 978-1-03-293097-8 (pbk)
ISBN: 978-1-315-86847-9 (ebk)

DOI: 10.4324/9781315868479

Typeset in Plantin
by Taylor & Francis Books

Contents

Citation Information vii
Notes on Contributors ix

1. Introduction: Islam, culture and women
Firdous Azim 1

2. Islamist women of Hamas: between feminism and nationalism
Islah Jad 7

3. Just between us: identity and representation among Muslim women
Amina Jamal 33

4. *'Bahar Nikalna'*: Muslim women negotiate post-conflict life
Diia Rajan, Deepa Dhanraj and K. Lalita 45

5. Piety, music and gender transformation: reconfiguring women as culture bearing markers of modernity and nationalism in Bangladesh
Samia Huq 57

6. The visibility of a pious public
Rianne Subijanto 73

7. Women, Islam and nation in Bengal
Firdous Azim 87

8. Popular expressions and matters of faith
Safia Azim 93

Index 105

Citation Information

The following chapters were originally published in the journal *Inter-Asia Cultural Studies*, volume 12, issue 2 (June 2011). When citing this material, please use the original page numbering for each article, as follows:

Chapter 2
Islamist women of Hamas: between feminism and nationalism
Islah Jad
Inter-Asia Cultural Studies, volume 12, issue 2 (June 2011) pp. 176-201

Chapter 3
Just between us: identity and representation among Muslim women
Amina Jamal
Inter-Asia Cultural Studies, volume 12, issue 2 (June 2011) pp. 202-212

Chapter 4
'Bahar Nikalna': *Muslim women negotiate post-conflict life*
Diia Rajan, Deepa Dhanraj and K. Lalita
Inter-Asia Cultural Studies, volume 12, issue 2 (June 2011) pp. 213-224

Chapter 5
Piety, music and gender transformation: reconfiguring women as culture bearing markers of modernity and nationalism in Bangladesh
Samia Huq
Inter-Asia Cultural Studies, volume 12, issue 2 (June 2011) pp. 225-239

Chapter 6
The visibility of a pious public
Rianne Subijanto
Inter-Asia Cultural Studies, volume 12, issue 2 (June 2011) pp. 240-253

Chapter 7
Women, Islam and nation in Bengal
Firdous Azim
Inter-Asia Cultural Studies, volume 12, issue 2 (June 2011) pp. 254-258

Chapter 8
Popular expressions and matters of faith
Safia Azim
Inter-Asia Cultural Studies, volume 12, issue 2 (June 2011) pp. 259-270

Notes on Contributors

Firdous Azim is Professor of English and Chairperson of the Department of English and Humanities at BRAC University in Bangladesh. She is a member of Naripokkho, a woman's activist organization based in Bangladesh. She is a member of the editorial collective of IACS. Her research interests and writings include post-colonial and feminist literary analysis and issues pertaining to feminist activism. She is the author of *The Colonial Rise of the Novel* (1993).

Safia Azim obtained her Bachelor's and Masters' degrees in Psychology from the University of Dhaka (Bangladesh), graduating at the top of her class in both instances and going on to a decade-long stint as faculty member. During this period, she also conducted cutting-edge research on violence against women as a member of the feminist organization, Naripokkho. Her passion for design led her to establish a unique and successful clothing brand, 'Kushaal'. Side-by-side she undertook several gardening and landscaping projects for both indoor and outdoor, public and privately-owned spaces. In 2003, she decided to pursue her inclination to work in the area of visual arts as a self-taught photographer-cum-graphic designer on a fulltime basis. Since 2004, she has been designing the artwork for CD inlays of musical albums of several Bangladeshi musicians, as well as some of their promotional material – posters, flyers, advertisements in both print-based and audio-visual media, as well as conceptualizing and overseeing the production of a number of music videos. This experience introduced her to a whole new world of digital equipment and editing software. Today, her Nikon D300 is her constant companion and her 'mechanical' third eye.

Deepa Dhanraj, President of Yugantar, is a noted filmmaker and has made over 50 documentaries and training films in the last 25 years. Her films have won awards in many international film festivals. Deepa has taught video-filming to women activists from South-East Asia, and has extensively lectured in various fora all over the country. She has been actively involved with the women's movement since 1980 on issues related to women's status, political participation, health and education. Her areas of interest are education and health, and in the last few years her work has focused on problems faced by children who are first generation learners from disadvantaged communities.

Samia Huq is an anthropologist and Assistant Professor at the Department of Economics and Social Science at BRAC University, Dhaka. She obtained her PhD from Brandeis University, USA, looking at women's religious discussion groups in urban Bangladesh. Her areas of interest include religious revival, religious identity, religion, politics, social movements and secularism. Publications from this research are on-going, appearing in several international peer reviewed journals and as book chapters. As part of the research team of the Pathways of Women's Empowerment RPC, Dr. Huq is currently involved in a book project tracing the cultural history of the Bengali Muslim woman as she lived in and created the world of Bengali performance arts in the context of partitions and the emergence of Bangladesh. Her other concurrent research is on Islamist women and their contribution to public debates and public policy issues.

Islah Jad is the Director of the Women's Studies Institute. She is Assistant professor of gender and development at Bir Zeit University, one of the founders of the Women's Studies Institute at Bir Zeit University and one of the founders of WATC (Women's Affairs Technical Committee), a national coalition for women. She has published many works on Palestinian and Arab women's political participation. She is the co-author for the Arab Human Development Report of 2005.

Amina Jamal is an Associate Professor of Sociology at Ryerson University, Toronto. She teaches courses in classical and contemporary social theory, race and ethnicity, Canadian immigration and women and Islam. Jamal's work has been published in *Signs*, *Meridians*, *Feminist Review* and the *Journal of Middle Eastern Women's Studies*. Her book on the cultural and political activism of Jamaat-e-Islami women in Pakistan is expected to be published in 2013. This book is based on an ethnographic and textual study of Jamaat women and it seeks to provide a much needed South Asian perspective to the otherwise useful studies of Islamist women in Egypt, Iran and other Muslim societies. She is presently engaged in a three-year research study funded by the Social Sciences and Humanities Research Council of Canada(SSHRC) on Muslim feminists' understanding of the secular as a cultural-historical experience of gendered politics in Muslim South Asia.

Dr K. Lalita, Secretary of Yugantar, is well known as a co-author and editor of classics in women's studies, such as *We Were Making History* (Kali For Women), *Women Writing in India from 600 BC to the 20th Century* (The Feminist Press) and *Taking Charge of Our Bodies* (Penguin). She was founder-president of India's first women's activist group, the Progressive Organisation of Women, and founder-coordinator and currently the Vice-President of the well-known Anveshi Research Centre of Women's Studies. She works on issues of gender, social justice, women's health and education.

Diia Rajan is a Research Associate with Yugantar, Hyderabad, where she is currently researching postconflict trauma and social recovery, specifically with Muslim youth in Hyderabad. For the past five years she has worked on issues of citizenship and development, and recently coordinated a multi-centred research project entitled 'Minority Women Negotiating Citizenship'. Prior to joining Yugantar, she worked with the Women's Rights and Citizenship initiative of the International Development Research Centre, Canada. Diia holds a BA in Political Science and an MA in Culture Studies from Canada and India. Her areas of interest include post-conflict life, gender, social policy and qualitative methodologies.

Rianne Subijanto is a graduate of University of Indonesia (BA) and New York University (MA). She is currently pursuing her PhD degree in media studies at the School of Journalism and Mass Communication at the University of Colorado, Boulder, USA. Her research focuses on Indonesia, media and modernity, including analyses of Islam and popular culture, of broadcasting industries and cultural policy and of the political economy of post-colonial Indonesia. Her publications include 'Indonesian Islamist media: a struggle against or a legitimacy of the dominant ideology?' in Thao Le (ed.) *Critical discourse analysis: An interdisciplinary perspective* (2009); and 'Producing a religious TV series: the making of a popular piety culture in Indonesia' in *Monograph in media anthropology, DIGITHUM Journal* (2009).

The chapters in this book were originally published in the journal *Inter-Asia Cultural Studies. Inter-Asia Cultural Studies* is supported by Chiang Ching-Kuo Foundation (ROC), Northeast Asian History Foundation and National Chiao Tung University, Taiwan.

Introduction: Islam, culture and women

Firdous Azim

The opening up of religious discourses and a new public presence of religion has forced cultural analyses and studies to take a fresh look at the ways in which religion enters social and cultural life. Especially after 9/11, there has been a political resurgence of religion and the presence of religion in the public space is strongly felt. While most discussions of Islam have concentrated on the political sphere, especially with the two wars that have plagued parts of the Asian continent during the last decade, this collection of articles concentrates on the way that Islam impacts on the everyday aspects of lives of people who reside in what can be designated as Muslim societies, or in communities where Islam plays a big part.

This book is part of the 'special issues' series, which puts together special issues of Routledge journals into books. This book thus springs out of a special issue entitled *Complex Terrains: Islam, culture and women in* Asia, published in *Inter-Asia Cultural Studies* in June of 2011. The journal issue itself had drawn on presentations made at an Inter-Asia Cultural Studies conference held in 2009 in Tokyo entitled 'Women Negotiating Islam'. The initial emphasis on negotiation is worth revisiting, as those presentations had looked at how women in different locations cope with the ways that religion, either as politics or as culture, enters their lives. In some cases, Islam is lived as policy, such as in the case of law and legal measures; in others it becomes a part of the state, such as when an Islamic party forms the government; in still others, it is part of a political discourse, as Islam-based parties seek to recruit women. While these negotiations take place in the public arena of government and policy, there are other spaces where the religion makes itself felt in indirect ways. This is the arena we have identified as the cultural, and women have had to negotiate, for example, with the strict codes that a more 'fundamentalist' approach to Islam makes on women's cultural activities. However, the cultural presence of Islam has made inroads more insidiously through popular culture such as music, television and art. These are some of the topics that this book takes on board, and it is hoped that readers will open the forum for more diverse ways of looking at how global politics influences and transforms everyday events, shapes our thinking, and the way that we negotiate and transform our own spaces.

The emphasis on the word negotiation helps to draw attention to an on-going process, which is dictated not by external pressures only, but traces a long history of women's engagement with Islam in diverse locations. This engagement had involved protest against the obvious misogynist aspects that Islam is (in)famous for, but also illustrates women's ambiguous positioning, situated as they are at the crossroads between modernity, tradition and nationalism. The papers presented looked at the way in which institutional structures such as the law empower (or not) women's lives, as well as the ways in which religion is practiced and manifested in everyday life. The emphasis was on women's active engagement with a new or traditional religious discourse, and ways in which new forms of feminine and feminist subjectivities may emerge from within these engagements.

Before going to talk about the articles in this book, a small reiteration on the importance of looking at the relationship between women and Islam is necessary. Since the publication of Edward Said's *Orientalism* in 1978, the cultural dimension of colonialism has become evident to all cultural analysts, and the special role that women have played in this process has been highlighted in all subsequent writing. The colonial representation of Islam had fixed on the figure of the veiled woman as emblematic of all that was wrong with Muslim societies. The colonized oriental, caught within this discourse, got enmeshed in discovering other forms of representation, often going to 'pre'-Islamic times to discover how great the position of women was 'originally'. This search for a golden age often pitches on the early years of Islam, to show how the times of the Prophet Muhammad had been good for women – that the new religion had given women rights, such as of property and of consent, which had hitherto been denied to them.[1] Most postcolonial histories give women this special status.[2] Women emerge as the nationalist response to the colonial representation. But while women become the terrain on which national and post-colonial identities are drawn, lives and voices of women are drowned. This is perhaps one of the reasons that women's groups and the women's movement have remained as dynamic and creative in the so-called Third World, as women contest and negotiate between the positions that are made available to them, and as they struggle to carve their own spaces.

'Muslim' societies, even when limited to Asia, are varied, and the enmeshing of issues of nationalism, anti-colonial and anti-imperial struggles are played out in very diverse and often incomparable terrains. The complexity of the relationship between Islam and women and the differences in the negotiating strategies that spring out of the differences in the contexts in which these struggles take place, need to be studied in more detail. Let us just take the case of Bangladesh as an instance. The emergence of Bangladesh as a nation state can perhaps be traced back to the early twentieth century, a period which had witnessed the growth and rise of a new professional middle class, which was at the time involved in forging for itself a sense of national identity, albeit under the aegis of British colonialism. However reading the cultural texts of this period – novels, articles, poems and plays - we will find that the newly-emerging Bengali middle class was divided or crucially differed along religious or communal lines. In the cultural field this difference manifested itself through the publication of 'Muslim'-edited journals, which ranged from the overtly religious to the more 'progressive' or 'secular' ones. As Muslim writers, both male and female, took up the pen, there began a lively and interesting debate on the place of the Bengali Muslim in the newly-emerging Bengali polity.

The political ramifications of this phenomenon acquired both class and religion-based or communal overtones. The Muslim League founded in 1906 spoke for the more urban-based Muslim, and had pan-Indian links, whereas more rooted parties, such as the Krishak Praja party, asserted the voice of the peasantry, who were identified as Muslim, and opposed to the land-owning or professional urban-based mainly Hindu middle class. In this morass of class and religious interests, the issue of women's positioning came to the fore. As mentioned earlier, Islam has always been castigated for its misogyny, and the 'backwardness' of the Bengali Muslim woman was associated with Islamic dictates, even as the 'new' woman was emerging from within its folds. Women writers debated the positioning of the Bengali Muslim woman in the newly-emerging nation state[s]. However what is most interesting about women's writing in early twentieth century Bengal, is that it often goes beyond communal and class interests, as writers such as the celebrated Rokeya Sakhawat Hossain (1880-1932) and who is often considered the forerunner of the feminist movement in Bangladesh talk about women's emancipation and empowerment and craft wonderful utopian visions where women rule in peace and harmony.

The case of Bengal is of interest as it provides an example of a constant veering between the poles that constitute a sense of modernity and nationhood. On the one hand, there is an appeal to a 'Bengali' culture, which is again difficult to identify. There is the 'genteel' or gentle middle-class cultural sphere (often referred to as the *bhadra* class), and the more peasant-based rural or folk culture. Emphasis on the rural draws inspiration not only from the water and soil, but valourises people's 'beliefs' and 'lifestyles', where an emphasis on religion as well as religious differences between Hindu and Muslim, are drawn on. The struggles for national independence and nation formation have oscillated between these poles, with Bangladesh, which emerged as East Pakistan as British rule departed in 1947, opting to be part of Pakistan on purely religious grounds. But as the struggle during the Pakistan years amply proves, commonality of religion did not provide enough ground to form a nation. When Bangladesh emerged in 1971 after a prolonged and finally bloody confrontation against the Pakistani state, it asserted secular and Bengali cultural bases for its formation. However contradictions remain, as is witnessed not only in the ideological veering between Bengali and Islamic principles as the foundations of the state, but even in the geographical boundaries that delineate the state, which had been drawn, in 1947, to demarcate Muslim majority areas outside the boundaries of the Indian state.

In this constant veering between diverse positions, women have again become a linchpin of national identity. The cultural representation of women has taken on many interesting dimensions, and is visible in women's clothes, for instance. As more women step out into the public their attire ranges from the traditional *burqa* to the more contemporary and fashionable *hijab*, where the head gear and the covering dress are colour-coded and matched. Women wear the South Asian *salwar kameez* in manifold styles, and the sari, which was considered the main emblem of a Bengali woman, has now to vie with many other styles, which claim cultural specificity and relevance. The negotiation or the struggle with religion – Islam – has in this case spawned many interesting images of women, and women are seen to actively negotiate and carve out spaces for themselves in various arenas, ranging from nation-formation and identity to political struggle, to literature and culture, and in everyday matters of dress, conduct and appearance.

The focus in this book is thus on the complexity of the negotiations between Islam, women and the nation, as well as on the interesting spheres that such an engagement has opened up. The focus on the cultural aspects that lie behind this negotiation draws in the political engagement as well; and ambiguities of positioning point to a very dynamic process. While the overtly political is easier to delineate, the ambiguities of the cultural lend themselves to different interpretations and readings. The cultural aspects of Islam have sometimes been seen as a form of self-assertion, but more often than not as part of an insidious entry into people's lives, which corrodes the building of a secular and modern society, towards which postcolonial 'third world' nations are supposed to be progressing.

Again, perhaps a word on modernity and secularism needs to be put in at this point. As the experience of Bangladesh traced above demonstrates, the construction of an Islamic public space is sometimes seen as inimical to the construction of a modern secular polity. The relationship between Islam and the nation needs to be teased out to highlight the underlying theme of modernity. Contemporary approaches to Islam further position the fundamentalist against the spiritual, the political against the cultural, and the western search for a 'moderate' Islam often selects the second term of these binaries as desirable. Hence, the construction of the Islamic public or cultural space comes under attack in two ways: one, as a handmaiden of contemporary western imperialist forces who, by patronizing a mild form of the religion, keep its more militant aspects at bay, or by the secularists, who consider the Islamicization of public spaces as inimical to the establishment of a tolerant pluralist society and as retarding the development of a more critical public space. Cultural expressions work by creating popular appeal, and it is difficult to decipher to what extent it reflects, and to what level constructs, this field of what has become known as the popular pious. However, the contemporary advent of Islam into the political and cultural sphere is engaged in its own negotiation with modernity, and taking on as it does the discourse of rights and justice, vies for a new placement within the modern.

The articles in this book span a wide geographical expanse, covering all of Asia, and show how women, culture and religion form a difficult and complex terrain in which political and social lives are lived. Political engagement is the focus of the first two articles, as Islah Jad shows how Hamas has opened up new forms of political engagement for women in Palestine, complicating the secular nature of the liberation struggle. Though the presence of Hamas has had a long history by now, and as the political realities of the region undergo rapid changes, Islah Jad's article shows how women have been drawn into Islamic political groups and tries to examine the attractions that such a movement may have for women, and the kind of political involvement it calls for. This becomes even clearer in Amina Jamal's contribution from Pakistan, which shows how religious parties, such as the Jamaat-e-Islami, recruit and form their appeal for women. The situation in India acquires quite different proportions, as is explored by Diaa Rajan, Deepa Dhanraj and K. Lalita, as women in post-riot Gujarat negotiate public spaces. These papers have looked at women in the line of fire, as it were, and the urgency of their situations requires focus and attention.

The more cultural and perhaps more difficult arenas to identify are brought up in the subsequent papers from Bangladesh and Indonesia. Samia Huq shows how the growing influence of Islam makes women turn away from cultural performances, such as singing and dancing. This in a country like Bangladesh is really a very novel phenomenon, where women's presence in the sphere of cultural performance had become an emblem of Bengali culture in the fight for the independence of Bangladesh, and a strong marker of difference from the Pakistani state. Rianne Subijanto considers TV drama serials and talk shows on Indonesian TV. The collusion between the popular public space and the state itself is shown to create a changing cultural scene in which religion acquires a huge and unmistakable presence. The visual essay concentrates on street scenes in and around Dhaka in Bangladesh. It reveals a completely different picture, concentrating on popular street art and building forms, as they construct a pious public image, and draw its viewers through a collage of aesthetic forms – folk and cinema. These forms remain outside the purview of any official patronage, and can be seen as true expressions of popular religion.

As editor, putting this book together has been a challenging task. It has had different avatars: as a panel presentation in a conference, as a special issue in a journal and finally as a book. The effort has been to draw on writers and articles that span a broad range of topics and concerns, and hope to elicit debate and discussion, and also add to the rich scholarship that has sprung out of activism, and continues to influence the movements in which many of our countries are engaged.

Notes

1 Cf Ahmed (1992).
2 See specially Sangari and Vaid (1988).

References

Ahmed, Leila (1992) *Women and Gender in Islam,* New Haven: Yale University Press.
Sangari, Kumkum and Vaid, Sudesh (1988) *Recasting Women: Essays in Colonial History,* New Delhi: Kali for Women.

Islamist women of Hamas: between feminism and nationalism

Islah JAD

ABSTRACT *In December, 1995, when Hamas announced the establishment of the Islamic National Salvation Party, a political organisation separate from its military wing, it opened the way for involvement of the Islamic movement in the political processes brought about in the West Bank and Gaza with the signing of the Oslo Accords and the arrival of the Palestinian National Authority. In speaking of the rights of different groups, including women, in its founding statement, and in setting up in Gaza a Women's Action Department, the new Party opened its doors to the 'new Islamic woman' and to a significant evolution in Islamist gender ideology in Gaza, if not in the West Bank – where, due to Hamas' policy there of targeting only males, there exists no parallel to the Salvation Party or organisational support for women like that represented by the Women's Action Department in Gaza. Hamas' gender ideology, like that of the secularist parties, remains contradictory, and doors to women's equality only partly open; nevertheless, Islamist women have managed to build impressive, well-organised women's constituencies among highly educated and professional women coming from poor and refugee backgrounds; and the Salvation Party shows an increasing tendency to foster gender equality and more egalitarian social ideals, while holding fast to the agenda of national liberation. These advances have been achieved both through alternative interpretations of Islamic legal and religious texts, and through positive engagement with the discourses of other groups, whether secular feminists or nationalists. In contrast, secularists are losing ground by advocating a discourse of rights in isolation from the national agenda and in the absence of a mobilising organisation. These developments suggest possibilities for mutual accommodation between Islamist and other Palestinian groups. They suggest also that the nature of the state proposed by Islamists will depend to a large extent on the visions and challenges posed by other nationalist and secularist groups.*

Conflict over the construction of gender and the ideal woman is neither a neutral nor a primarily religious concern. Islamists, just like nationalists, seek to establish an ideal society that depends upon a particular conception of the ideal woman (Kandiyoti 1991, 1996; Moghadam 1994; Papanek 1994). The difference between the two – and the problems this poses for women – arises from the dedication of religious or fundamentalist groups to the restoration of an ideal past or a mythical age that allocates to women to the role of guardian of traditions (Zubaida 1997, 2000, 2003; Roy 1999).

Visions of such a past typically place strong emphasis on the role women are imagined to have played in infusing life with perfection. In this sense, the ideal woman embodies a past time evoking the 'traditional family and moral values on which our nation' (Hawley 1994: 32) was built. Such a vision causes fundamentalist groups to be seen as actively helping to make 'traditional' gender roles second nature in fundamentalist religion (Hawley 1994: 34). The 'traditional' Islamist ideal woman comes to be viewed as opposed to the 'modern' ideal woman constructed in nationalist secularist discourse

(Hawley 1994: 30; White 2002). In the eyes of those who do not share this vision, the ideal society that Islamists strive to build is reactionary and anti-modern (Al-Azmeh 1996; Zubaida 1997; Roy 1999).

The ongoing debate between secularists and Islamists in the Middle East reinforces the dichotomy. Secularism, for Islamists, is a colonial imposition, a worldview that gives precedence to the material over the spiritual and results in a culture of alienation and unrestrained hedonism. Secularism, for secularists, is central to universal humanism, a rational principle that calls for the suppression, or at least the restraint, of religious passion so that a dangerous source of intolerance and delusion can be controlled, and political unity, peace and progress secured (Al-Messiri and Al-Azmeh 2000, cited in Asad 2003: 21).

I aim to problematise this exclusionary dichotomy between Islamists and nationalist secularists. By focusing on the Women's Action Department in the Salvation Party, the party established by Hamas as its political wing in the post-Oslo period, I examine the formal gender ideology of the Islamic movement Hamas and show how this formal ideology is reconstructed, re-narrated and practised by Islamist women. As I argue throughout this paper, the formal ideology of Palestinian Islamists largely stems not from religious texts but from accommodation to contending positions. The 'traditions' that the Islamist, like the modernist nationalist, seeks to revive are 'invented' and, like those of the nationalist, are modern constructs (Hobsbawm 1983: 2–3).

In this paper, I refrain from using the term 'feminist' to denote all forms of women's activism, as does Badran (1994: 204). I agree that women's activism opens up new spaces for women that might contradict prevailing gender roles. I shall also refrain from using the label 'feminist' to refer to Islamist women, since many of the women the term might seek to represent refuse to identify with it. The changes that these women seek to implement are contingent upon various circumstances that might not always challenge gender imbalances. At times, they may even support patriarchal structures. Islamist women regard feminism as superfluous (Badran 1994: 203), anti-male, and even indicative of some sort of 'genetic deformation'.[1] Furthermore, in the course of my interviews, I realised that Islamists attentively read and follow what feminists write about them. A similar controversy arises over the term 'fundamentalist'.[2] Women in Islamic movements see this term as alien, politically loaded, Western, irrelevant and integral to colonialist strategies to undermine the indigenous social and religious culture (Karam 1998: 6; Al-Huda Association 1998). Throughout this paper I refer to 'Islamists' as they would to themselves and to their movement as the Islamic movement.

Hamas was formed during the first *intifada*, when, on 9 December 1987, the Muslim Brothers in Palestine reincarnated themselves as the Islamic Resistance Movement, or Hamas, thereby creating a resistance force separate from and outside the Palestine Liberation Organisation. The new force was able to compete with the national movement led by Yasser Arafat and his Fateh Party. During the *intifada*, Hamas employed peaceful means, only adopting military tactics from 1992 onwards, after Yasser Arafat signed the Oslo Accords (El-Hamad and Al-Bargothi 1997; Hroub 2000). Soon afterward, in order to function as a political, as well as an ideological and military, movement in the post-Oslo period, Hamas separated its military wing from its political organisation. On 11 December 1995, Hamas announced the establishment of the *Hizb al-Khalas al-Watani al-Islami* – the Islamic National Salvation Party, or Salvation Party, with the Arabic acronym *'Khalas'* (INSP 1995). This was a significant development. It allowed Hamas to participate in the debates and political processes brought about by the arrival of the Palestinian National Authority, to play a part in the development of (what was hoped would be) a new state, and to give these efforts priority along with the national struggle for freedom from Israeli colonial rule and military occupation. This party, the political arm of Hamas, is no longer in existence today but it functioned in Gaza as a legal opposition party. Despite plans to establish its headquarters in Jerusalem, it operated in Gaza only; it was not active in the West Bank or East Jerusalem.

In its founding statement, the Party used, for the first time in the history of the Muslim Brothers Movement in Palestine, the language of 'rights' for different social groups, in particular for women and other disadvantaged groups, such as labourers, which had rarely been targeted by the Brothers' activism. The Party statement stressed the need for participation in political-cultural activity and social-economic construction, including the need to protect religious values and civil rights – including those of labourers, cultural societies, and women. In what follows, I examine the position of women within the Salvation Party and the ways in which their roles differed from those played by nationalist and secularist women within the structure of the national movement. Throughout this paper, I reserve the term 'Islamist women' for those who belong to the Islamic movement and who are actively engaged through their activism in the public sphere in promoting what Keddie has called an 'Islamic state that would enforce at least some Islamic laws and customs' (Keddie 1998; Karam 1998: 16).

Demobilisation in mobilisation: Hamas' gendered structure in the West Bank

In this section I analyse the contradiction between the marginalisation of women in Hamas' organisational structure and their mobilisation in civil society in the West Bank. Islamist women were a crucial force in broadening Hamas constituencies in the student movement, but their activism was not recognised within the movement structure in the West Bank, as Hamas' structure for the inclusion of women differs in the West Bank from that in Gaza. I argue that this gendered form of structure might have been an important factor in demobilising women outside Gaza, especially when Hamas became a hegemonic political power in the Palestinian polity during and in the aftermath of the first Palestinian *intifada*. The Salvation Party established in Gaza has no parallel body in the West Bank. Nor does Hamas have in the West Bank any mobilising and organising structures for other social groups, such as students or workers. While male party members participated in the different activities of the *intifada* (organising strikes, funeral processions, confrontations with the Israeli army and so on), female Hamas members at the time were not visible as participants. (Veiled women participants were not necessarily Islamists.) The reason for this absence can be explained by the fact that Islamist organisations in the West Bank target only males. I found no indication in documents or interviews that women were participants or were targeted for recruitment either as voters or as candidates. Nor did the activism shown by Islamist women in universities flow from the organisational structure of Hamas; it was due, rather, to the efforts of the female students themselves, competing for votes in university elections. In the West Bank, once a female student leaves the university, she has no place to go in the structure of the movement. Originally, the same situation applied to Gaza, where the growing number of female students at the Islamic University, and later, from Al-Azhar University or other colleges, had no place to go except to work in the social institutions belonging to the Muslim Brothers. It was in late 2003 that the Hamas leaders announced their intention to form an Islamic women's movement, and female students joined forces with mainstream political organisations such as the Salvation Party. But this occurred only in Gaza.

Organising students and linking them to political parties is crucial in Palestine, where youth in general, and students in particular, play an important role in boosting the national movement and the struggle against the Occupation. An attempt to answer why Islamists in the West Bank did not seek to organise female students in their mainstream political parties – whether under the name of the Muslim Brothers, Hamas or the Salvation Party – must acknowledge that these institutions carried the imprint of the conservative gender ideology familiar to the Islamist movement from its inception. This was especially true when it came to young unmarried females.

According to activists in the Islamic student movement: 'We can ask for a big mixed meeting in the universities for both sexes when we have a common goal to achieve, such as a major protest against the university administration or a flagrant violation of our right as an Islamic bloc to organise our activities, but we don't have a mixed structure for students' (Ahmed, Amira, Youssra, Interviews).

The lack of such structures affects female graduates severely in the West Bank, where the number of Islamist institutions is more limited and scattered than in Gaza. In the West Bank, women have available to them only a few charitable societies. Typical examples are the al-Huda Islamic society, Al-Khansa'a society (both in al-Bireh and in Ramallah), Hanieen in Nablus, the Muslim Woman's Society in Jerusalem and a similar one in Hebron. These organisations are very similar to the old type of women's charitable society that existed during the British Mandate. They usually have a central figure as a director (*modeera*), an administrative committee (*hayaa idareyya*) of 5–11 members, elected from a general assembly (*hayaa 'amah*) of 100–300 members. Like the old charitable societies, their focus is not on organising women but on providing a limited number of work opportunities in home economies, such as embroidery and catering. In providing catering, these societies proved serious competition for the many women's societies, old and new, which had managed to establish a 'web of relations with the PA ministries, banks and many private enterprises' (Samira, Interview). According to the directors of these societies, the financial revenues of their activities cover their expenses. In addition, they manage to attract important donations from Islamist businessmen who see their activities as in line with the rules of Islam to support the poor, orphans, prisoners' and martyrs' families, and the needy in general. These societies receive no foreign funding, which gives them legitimacy when they attack and de-legitimise other women's organisations, in particular those working with women's NGOs.

The Islamist women's charitable societies also organise alternative cultural activities, separate from those of nationalist and feminist women's groups. International Women's Day, an international festival celebrated on 8 March every year, is replaced by the Festival of the Muslim Woman (*mahrajan al-marah al-moslema*). The day is picked for a 'pragmatic' reason, before the end of the academic school and university year. According to Samira, 'this is to get the help of female students in organising the festival; otherwise it would be difficult later on to find them or bring them together' (Samira, Interview). These festivals usually attract a huge number of women and their children: Samira estimated 2000–2500 women. These rallies are an extension of the usual proselytising of the Muslim Brothers (*nashr al-d'awa*) when they urge women to comply with the rules of their religion and encourage them to be good committed Muslims (*moltazema*). Again, as in the old type of women's charitable societies, women who attend these rallies are not asked to undertake any political activity in a party organisation.

The view of the Brothers in the West Bank that women's role is mainly in the domestic sphere prevents their organising women after graduation. As Ahmed puts it:

> Women after graduation have no place to go, and this is because of the prevailing conservative vision in our 'oriental' society. But also, in the thinking of many Islamists, a woman's role is still limited to her home and family, so the focus and expectation after graduation is that women will go to their homes. This is the rule among Islamists in the West Bank. Any exception will depend fully on the women's husband's wish after marriage, to allow her to be active or not; and many choose not to. (Ahmed, Interview)

The absence of mobilising structures for women Islamists in the West Bank contrasts with the coordination among male Islamists in the militant – and all-male – underground

Hamas structure in different regions of the West Bank. Islamist women are not part of the underground structure. (In fact, all Islamist women interviewed claimed to have no connection to Hamas.) There is no legal, official unifying Islamist structure, as in the case of the Salvation Party in Gaza. It was, however, difficult to determine whether the lack of any unifying body for Islamist women is simply a result of the organisation's internal priorities, or whether it stems from an utter lack of interest in organising Islamist women in the West Bank (in contrast to Gaza). When Islamist women in the West Bank were asked if they co-ordinated their activities or programmes, the answers were negative. However, the women asserted that 'when possible, we attend each others' rallies and conferences' (Maysoon, Interview).

Gaza: mainstreaming gender 'à la Islamism'

In this section, a thorough analysis of the Women's Action Department (established right along with the Party) of the Salvation Party will be provided in order to understand the ways in which Islamists incorporate women into politics as they create the image of the 'new Islamic woman' (White 2002). Islamist women are presented with the need to combine two paradoxical expectations: to live as model mothers and obedient wives, on the one hand, and to live as model political activists, on the other. It is the same dilemma that nationalist and secularist women are still struggling to solve.

Hamas' contradictory gender ideology, like that of the nationalists, stresses the accepted role of women in reproducing the nation. While the movement is keen to present the 'new Islamic woman', it is apparent that this image potentially contradicts the usual conception of the Palestinian woman as the fertile 'womb'.

The Party and its Women's Department opened their doors to the 'new Islamic woman', who is highly educated, outspoken, *moltazemah* and modern. Modernity is reflected in the fact that these women are educated, professional and politically active. The veil is seen as a signifier of modernity since it is different from 'traditional dress'. The 'new Islamic dress' (a long robe of plain colour and a white or black head scarf) is seen as:

> Different from the *thub* [traditional peasant woman's dress] which is used by our mothers and grandmothers. It is different in its meanings; it is a unifying symbol to our followers and members If I see a woman wearing it, I will immediately realise that she is *ukho*[3] [a sister]. It indicates that we are educated and not like our mothers, who are mostly illiterate. It gives us *heiba* [respect] like the dress of our *ulama* [religious clergy]. It is economic, simple and modest. (Amira, Youssra, Maysoon, and Kholod, Interviews)

In this view, Islamist dress is regarded as superior to the *thub* because it is a uniform of conviction, unlike the blind adherence to tradition that is presumed to explain clothing practices among the masses. Implicit in the Islamist veiling style is participation in a national social movement that lends the wearer a heightened sense of status, both moral (vis-à-vis secularists) and social (vis-à-vis women who merely cover, but do not veil). However, despite its political cachet, behind the social force of veiling, 'one can discern the familiar principle of *himaya* [guidance and protection], by [and from] men' (White 2002: 223).

Unlike some other Islamic parties, as in Turkey for example, in which Islamist women, once married, lose their 'voice' as they retreat to the security and seclusion of the patriarchal family (White 2002), the Salvation Party and its Women's Action Department make available an important venue for a category of women who are highly educated (BA and higher degrees) and at the same time have limited access to the restricted, male-dominated labour market. In this sense, it is important to trace the identity the Party provides for women so that they may manage their dual roles as activists in the public sphere and as mothers and caregivers in the domestic sphere.

While education is an important facilitator of class mobility, the fact that the majority of Islamist women are refugees, educated in Gazan universities or in universities in other Arab countries and possessing a 'conservative' outlook, limits their chances of employment. For example, the NGO sector, which functions as an important employer of educated women, requires proficiency in foreign languages, as well as managerial and administrative skills. In Gaza, the Salvation Party takes upon itself the role of a 'developmental party' to 'mainstream' gender in the Party structure at all levels, as will be shown.

The Women's Action Department, *'da'erat al 'amal al-nissaei'*, is one of 13 departments in the Party managing all aspects of activities and administration, ranging from public relations and cultural and political affairs to women's affairs. Unlike the women's organisations in the national movement, the Department was originally clandestine and therefore had to take a different form. The Women's Action Department of Hamas has been able to integrate women, not into a separate section, but fully into its political organs, whether in the leadership or in its popular base.

The popular base of the Salvation Party is represented in the General Conference, which is elected from amongst the Party members in the different regions. The General Conference elects the central *majlis al-shoura* (Consultative Council), consisting of men and women. The *majlis al-shoura* decides the general policy of the Party and is not merely consultative to the politburo, *al-maktab al-seyyassi*, which is also elected, but is a decision-making body. The *majlis al-shoura* of the Salvation Party is composed of 52 members. Of these, eight (15.3%) are women (elected by men and women in the General Conference) and of the eight, five are refugees, three are from Gaza City, five are married with children, and three are single. The elected women are highly educated graduates from Jordan, Egypt, Syria and Gaza, in physics, chemistry, medical science, education and English. None of them had belonged to an organised political party before they joined the Salvation Party. Only one woman in the *majlis al-shoura* and *al-maktab al-seyyassi* had male relatives in the Party, suggesting that women in the Women's Department mostly win the jobs on their own merit as educated activists.

In each region of Gaza, there is a five-member *hayaa ideareyya* (administrative committee). In each *hayaa* there are two heads – one for men and the other for women – who organise contacts and events. The women in these committees are not there to enforce segregation but rather are fully incorporated members of Party bodies. As Amira Haroun, head of the Women's Department, puts it,

> It is not about segregation; we've discussed this issue in the Party several times. It is because women previously didn't know the male candidates and vice versa. So at this level, women members vote for women and male members vote for men. Once all reach the General Conference, they all [males and females together] choose the male and female members for the *majlis al-shoura* and then the politburo. (Amira Haroun, Interview)

In the politburo, two women out of 13 (15.3%) are unmarried and were elected by men and women in the *majlis al-shura*. These percentages are much higher than those found in all political bodies in the Palestine Liberation Organisation (PLO) or in the Palestinian National Authority (PA), whether achieved through nomination or election. In the Palestinian National Council, for example, which is formed by nomination according to a party quota (in which Fateh holds the majority according to a formula in which it has to control more than half of the seats, or 50 + 1), women represent 7.5% (56 out of 744). There are no women representatives on the Executive Committee, the highest level of the PLO.[4] In contrast, the primary task of the Women's Action Department of the Salvation Party is to include women in public life through their involvement in Party activities. As the head of the Department put it: 'We have a yearly plan to *damj* [integrate] women, politically and culturally, into the society' (Amira Haroun, Interview). The Department is keen to increase women's membership in the Party, which, according to Amira Haroun and Youssra, constitutes about 27% of the General Conference.

In order to facilitate the integration process, the Party and its satellite societies run a massive web of kindergartens at minimal charge, and poorer women and wives of political prisoners are exempted from paying any fees. Running kindergartens was a common task during the first *intifada*, originally undertaken by nationalist and secularist women's organisations and later abandoned. The vacuum left by these organisations was not filled by the PA when it was established in 1993 but by Islamist organisations. By running a web of kindergartens, the Islamists solved a major problem for working mothers and women activists. However, it is important to note that the two women who managed to make it to the top level of the Party were both unmarried. Work in the politburo, according to Youssra and Amira, 'is intense and diversified, and needs lots of time and strong character'. The times set for political meetings, usually arranged for the convenience of men rather than women, were identified by many feminists as a hindrance to women's participation in political parties (Waylen 1996). However, when asked whether meeting times were suitable for women, the women cited the veil as a facilitator of their involvement, even during late hours. As they clarified:

> We have certain days to discuss our general plans within the Party in these meetings, and we choose collectively the best time for all of us, men and women. But even if we have to be late sometimes, this does not pose a problem for us: since we are *moltazemat* no one approaches us to do any harm. It is known that we work for the benefit of our people, and we are well respected for that. (Youssra and Amira, Interview)

In this case, the veil facilitates mobility for politically committed women, giving them the required validation for transcending the social taboos that ordinarily restrict unmarried women from moving during late hours. If the impetus to maintain one's virtue is located in behaviour, then behavioural signals, such as choice of dress, become important markers of the unapproachability and inviolability of Islamist women.

The Women's Action Department employs various strategies and methods for reaching and recruiting women. They work face to face, building cells in refugee camps as entry points. Their task is facilitated by the presence of large numbers of political prisoners to whom they give special attention in their activities. They also include the prisoners' families. The Department organises a yearly campaign on behalf of political prisoners (now forgotten by almost all nationalist and secular women's organisations), in the form of demonstrations against Israel and the Palestinian Authority. The demonstrations against the latter take place because of the PA's 'lack of democracy and to oppose the continuous harassment against the Party offices and its journal, along with the arrest of its leaders'[5] (Youssra and Amira, Interview).

While Islamist ideology and activism does open doors for women, these tend to be revolving doors for the less-educated women, who are often unable to sustain an activist or professional life or to support themselves or their families. Many of these women are wives of political prisoners. (A large majority of Palestinian political prisoners are from the Islamic movement.) When asked what the Department does for these women, leaders answered:

> We try our best to attract these women to our activities. We organise workshops for them, to train them in different professions to sustain themselves. But in many cases these women withdraw. They are pressured by their imprisoned husbands not to enrol in the courses or to leave their homes, especially if the men have been sentenced for long periods. We could not do anything to help; this is a sensitive family matter. (Youssra, Interview)

When asked if they use their power within the party to pressure their husbands to change their mind about women's participation, the women replied in the negative. This reaction can be attributed to the contradictory values promoted by the Islamists' Party

–political and social involvement versus motherhood, family unity, and obedience to husbands.

To deal with specific women's issues, the Department annually organises a one-day women's conference, in which men and women participate by presenting papers on subjects relating to gender. The papers either cover 'hot topics' already placed on the national agenda by secular nationalist women's groups, or treat specific problems that women face in their respective fields of activity, such as employment, political life and culture. Some workshops are directed at male members of the Department and focus on topics such as socialisation or involve thorough discussion of *shari'a*, or family law. According to Amira: 'Some topics elicit fierce resistance from men, as in the discussion of *shari'a*, while other topics, like mixing [male and female], are contested and some male members are provoked by the separation between the sexes in our activities' (Amira Haroun, Interview). As one male member of the Party put it, 'As a Party keen for the development of women, we should abolish segregation in the Party' (Zeyyad, Interview).

The attitude of the Salvation Party and Islamist women concerning *shari'a* will be dealt with more fully later, but it is important to note here that the motivation behind the call to reform *shari'a* is in essence an effort to change internal power relations between males and females within the family structure. Male members are receptive to change and support 'mixing', which enhances the image of the Party and its women as 'modern', while at the same time they continue to object to significantly deeper and less 'visible' changes within the family. Support for mixing is not shared by all Islamists, many of whom encourage segregation among students in the university, suggesting that they believe that even veiling is insufficient to allow women to transcend sex barriers.

Since the conferences are a vehicle for presenting Islamist ideology on gender, it is noteworthy that the highest level of Hamas leadership is keen to attend the women's conferences 'to show their support' for what women do. Sheikh Ahmed Yassine (one of the founders of the old generation of Muslim Brothers in Palestine and a founder and the spiritual head of Hamas, assassinated by Israel in 2004) was keen to attend and gave a speech at the first women's conference in 1998. At the second women's conference in 1999, Mahmoud al-Zahhar, a prominent Hamas leader, attended and gave a paper – a precedent, as far as I know, in the history of the Palestinian women's movement to date.[6]

At the fifth conference (2003), Sheikh Ahmed Yassine was present, as was Dr Abdel Aziz Rantissi. The establishment of the 'Islamic Women's Movement in Palestine' was announced in the presence of more than 1500 men and women. With this 'Movement', the Islamists intended to link all Islamist women's institutions and thus coordinate and channel their efforts into representing the Islamic vision for women. The movement included nine women's groups: the Muslim Women's Association, The Women's Action Party in the Salvation Party, the Women's Action Department in *Al-mojam'a Al-Islami*, the Islamic bloc (female students), Female Student's Council in the Islamic University, the Palestinian Mothers' Society, Family Care Society, the Women's Unit in the Arab Institute for Study and Research, and the Mothers of Martyrs Society.

It is important to note that while the presence of the top leadership at the Islamist women's conference could be interpreted as encouraging women's public role and activism, their presence could also be interpreted as a potential for closure, a hardening of positions and a retreat into interpretations of Islam that might affect women negatively. The fifth conference, for example, was used to launch a massive attack on the proposed draft to reform the 'Penal Code' in favour of a more egalitarian approach in the penalties applied for adultery and the use of violence against women in the family. The old law discriminated against women by imposing harsher punishment on adulteresses in comparison with men, and was more tolerant in the case of domestic violence. In attacking the proposed draft, the leadership emphasised that the proposed reforms were not based on *shari'a*. This position represented an escalation in the male Islamists' demands, in its insistence that not only family law, but also the Penal Code, should be based on *shari'a*. Under their attack, the Palestinian parliament, the Legislative Council, halted discussion of the proposed reform.[7] At the same conference, and with the support of the Islamist women, the Islamist leadership exercised its power to stall an open and critical discussion on the proposed changes in the penal law, making it clear that the formal stand of the party followed the common view that *shari'a* is fixed and derived from sacred sources (Zubaida 2003: 1). However, this apparent 'freezing' of *shari'a* was to be subverted by Islamist women in their daily party activism and in their daily interactions with other women's groups.

Conflict had also erupted between the Islamists, on the one hand, and secularists and feminist women's organisations, on the other, over some parts of the proposed reform of the family law. In 1998, the Islamists had launched a sweeping campaign to halt any discussion of the proposed changes in the law. However, at that time Islamists did not have an organised women's movement. In the case of the Penal Code, the conflict would be settled less easily since the Islamist women's movement is well organised and well integrated into the Party structure.

In the above analysis, I have shown how women's representation was secured within the Islamic Salvation Party. The Women's Department was a catalyst for the inclusion of more women activists in the Party in order to widen its constituencies. In order to achieve this goal, it was necessary to take these women's needs into consideration. A web of kindergartens, as well as different programmes aiming at cadre formation and skill provision for different categories of women were important in facilitating this task. The Women's Department proved extremely successful in mobilising a large number of women to defend the party against PA harassment, in defending the Party line in preserving *shari'a* and in discrediting secularist and feminist women's groups also calling for legal reforms. In their activism, they borrowed a great deal from the secular women's organisations' modes of activism, employing similar types of projects, programmes and organisational forms.

The new participants brought into the Islamic movements by the Party included university graduates, professional women and future intellectuals, thus consolidating a new category that moved Hamas from a military, underground, male-dominated organisation into a more popular political movement. The move to create an Islamic women's movement with the support of the top leadership was a significant marker in the history of the Palestinian women's movements. For the first time, women became a strategic concern for the Palestinian national movement, this time under the banner of Islam. However, the birth of the Islamic women's movement occurred at a time when *shari'a* was seen as fixed, an attitude that effectively undermined women's call for more egalitarian treatment under the law.

The gender ideology of Hamas

While Hamas' gender ideology rests on religious tenets, it is, nonetheless, possible to demonstrate that it is contradictory and in continuous flux. This is due not only to Islamist women's activism within the Islamist movement, but also to 'ordinary' socio-economic factors and, as I have suggested, was a reaction to the challenge presented by the discourse of feminist nationalist and secular women. I have argued elsewhere (Jad 2004) that the universalist discourse used by women in NGOs was viewed by Islamist women as alien not because it was 'western', but because it was not founded on a thorough knowledge of the situation of the women whose interests these organisations claimed to be representing. This discourse was also reproduced and diffused in the absence of a power structure to support it – either in the Islamic women's movement or in the national secular political movement that developed in the aftermath of the Oslo Agreement.

The lack of attention to the study of gender ideology and its impact on gender relations in the study of Islamic movements in the Middle East by male scholars has been widely criticised. Examining the impact of the gender ideology of Hamas has, to some extent, been the task of some women writers (Taraki 1989; Hammami 1991, 1997; Milton-Edwards 1996; Pavlowsky 1998; Jad 2000). Cautioning against this neglect, Keddie warns that 'such studies are still considered something apart by most male scholars, and not as something that deeply affects politics and society so much that they cannot be dealt with adequately without taking cognisance of gender questions' (Keddie 1999: 17).

Bringing socio-economic factors into the debate, Moghadam notes that increases in female education and employment have slowly weakened the system of patriarchal gender relations, creating status inconsistency and anxiety on the part of the men of the petty bourgeoisie (Moghadam 1993: 137). In the same vein, Taraki, looking at modernisation in Jordan, argues that what has characterised the period after the middle of this century has been the breaking down of barriers that had kept women out of sight and therefore out of (the male) mind (Taraki 2003: 214). While women had always been physically visible in the fields and in the marketplace, they had occupied their place within a sexual division of labour that upheld the patriarchal order. The entry of women into the wage labour force, the educational system, and the public domain in general began to challenge the traditional order, especially as men and women not related to one another were thrust into work and other societal situations far from the observant eyes of the family.

Taraki explains that increasing economic need has forced men to acquiesce in women's seeking employment outside the home, and that state-sponsored mandatory education for women has meant that resistance to female education is no longer a viable option. Limited choices in these areas, therefore, are compensated for by ensuring that when women go out into the sexually integrated world, they do so with the minimum of social risk. She concludes that the Islamic movement in Jordan, in making women's dress and conduct a cornerstone of its social agenda, expresses what individual men feel: fear of losing control over 'their' women and the need to be assured that other men cannot lay a claim to them (Taraki 2003: 214). If this is the case, then the failed promises of post-independence developmentalism might be interpreted not as mere technical failures, according to Kandiyoti, but as moral failures requiring a complete overhaul of the worldviews underpinning them. Kandiyoti states that it is 'against this background that some oppositional movements have been advocating a "just" Islamic order, invoking notions of authentic Muslim womanhood as part of a broader critique of Westernisation and consumerism' (Kandiyoti 1996: 24).

Turning to Palestine, socio-economic and political factors have been invoked by many scholars to explain the spread of politicisation and mobilisation of women by national secular movements in the 1970s and the 1980s, which led to the massive participation of women in the first Palestinian *intifada* (Taraki 1989; Jad 1990; Kuttab 1993; Hammami 1997; Hasso 1997). The growing influence of Islamists, on the other hand, can only be explained with reference to a series of interrelated factors: the failure of the peace process, the decline of the Palestinian national movement, accompanied by the withdrawal of grassroots organizations from service provision; the 'NGOisation' of women's organisations, which ruptured their organic links with the grassroots; the 'nationalisation' of Islam; and the 'Islamisation' of the Palestinian national identity by the Muslim Brothers in Palestine.

Central to this latter process was the Islamisation of gender. Hammami has noted that the 1987 *intifada* was the first time 'that an issue, specifically veiling, once relegated to the arena of religious behaviour, had been mobilised as a nationalist issue' (Hammami 1997: 194). Hammami rightly points out this campaign showed the ability of Hamas to conflate its social ideology with Palestinian nationalism, wielding the threat and use of violence against women to impose the veil. In this struggle, women had little support from the national leadership of the *intifada*, which failed to confront the veiling campaign in time (Hammami 1997: 194).

In order to understand the gender agenda of Hamas, factors that link gender and nationalism must be explored. The gender ideology of Hamas cannot be separated from the colonial 'use' of gender, rivalry with 'other' nationalist groups and, to a lesser extent, scriptural texts. However, other factors, such as the conservative elements of Palestinian nationalism in its secular form, can be invoked to elucidate the slide into Hamas' gender ideology (Jad 1990; Budeiri 1995; Massad 1995; Hammami 1997).

I would argue that the orthodoxy[8] displayed by Hamas in the first *intifada* cannot be explained as a misreading of indigenous culture, as it arose in the context of a reaction to increasing intimidation of women, a circumstance aggravated by the Israeli Occupation. Hamas, contrary to Fateh, spelt out its gender agenda at an early stage. This is a common feature of religious movements that place a great deal of emphasis on the family unit. The Israeli writer Amnon Cohen, in his well-known work entitled 'The Moslem [sic] Brothers', said the movement had 'fixed repressive ideas about women and how they were expected to conduct themselves. Women were not permitted to use makeup or to over-adorn themselves, they were to veil their faces, and were not to appear in public "half naked". This, the Brothers maintained, was clearly laid down by Islam' (Cohen 1982). This strict gender agenda and moral system softened as it grew and became more popular. It also evolved in relation to the sort of pressure exercised by Islamist women on their leaders, which was heightened by the level of 'empowerment' these women achieved through their activism within the movement.

The moral nation needs moral women

Mohanty warns against the analytical leap of seeing the widespread practice of veiling as indicative of women's sexual oppression and control. Rather, she urges us to understand it by questioning its meaning and function in various cultural and ideological contexts (Mohanty 1991: 66–67). Hamammi showed that the spread of veiling in the course of the first *intifada* was linked to a national meaning – that in the face of the calamity, death and destruction inflicted by the Israeli Occupation, women had to show respect to the martyrs. She also blamed the leftist groups for not stopping the veiling campaign. In her argument, all women are put in a single category – women who refuse to adopt the veil, and women who are oppressed by it. This 'homogenisation of women, irrespective of their class, race, religious and daily material practices, might create a false sense of the commonality of oppressions, interests, and struggles between and among women' (Mohanty 1991: 68). This stance has resulted in the denial of agency and voice for Islamist women. I problematise the assumption by analysing how the old 'orthodoxy' of the Islamists is different from the 'new' one.

Contrary to claims made by authors such as Amnon Cohen, cited above, the intimidation of women is a kind of artefact of the Occupation rather than the result of a fixed conservative culture which 'oppresses women'. Hamas's focus on military activism should be highlighted to better explain its position vis-à-vis women's piety and veiling at any particular moment. Secondly, the veil has different meanings for different women according to their self-perception, class and ideology. In short, a more nuanced approach to the meaning of veiling is important in the elaboration of an oppositional political strategy.

During the first *intifada*, a new formulation of the issue of women's piety and modesty was deemed essential in order to 'protect' the nation. In fact, this formulation had been spelled out clearly a few years before the *intifada*, in secret booklets Hamas used to distribute to its male members to warn them against the interrogation and torture practices widely used in Israeli prisons. Hamas believed that the detailed confessions extracted from PLO prisoners, as weak secularists lacking faith, had brought disaster down on the armed struggle against Israel. It was feared that the Islamic endeavour would suffer a similar fate unless its disciples were taught to steel themselves against the worst physical and psychological pressure the Israelis could apply. Resistance, unyielding internal strength and empowerment were vital for withstanding torture and interrogation.[9] Between 1986 and 1987[10] the Brothers founded two military organisations in preparation for a military resistance: the Palestinian *mujahedeen* and *al-jihad wal da'wa* – with the acronym *'majd'* (glory). The latter was a highly secret organisation concerned with 'intelligence and pre-emption' (*istikhbarat wa rad'e*). It aimed at: protecting the movement from any penetration from the Israelis or other Palestinian organisations; collecting information on the Israelis; gathering information on any form of 'moral corruption' in the society, whether it was related to suspected collaborators, drug dealers, thieves, or prostitutes; increasing awareness on security matters through booklets and leaflets; and interrogating collaborators to punish them or 'liquidate them' (Abul-Omrein 2000: 197).

Before the *intifada*, this organisation took on the 'liquidation' of collaborators. In a booklet addressed to its militant members, the movement declared that those who proudly defied their interrogators would be rewarded as though they had died for the glory of Allah. But those who broke under interrogation would never know forgiveness, for they had done more harm than just damaging the organisation. In clear rivalry with other nationalist organisations, the movement sought to be more solid, moral, faithful, and empowered by God and religion. In this context, confessions under Israeli torture would present the organisation as weak and infiltrated, which will deter new candidates from joining the military wing and fail to distinguish Hamas from 'other less faithful' groups. It could not be claimed that Islam was superior to secularism unless the Hamas people were known to 'spit out their blood and teeth under the whip' (Schiff and Ya'ari 1989: 232). An iron will, the handbook preached, was all one needed to withstand deprivation, whippings, electric shocks, and threats: 'We must remember that the enemy's strength is naught compared with Allah's grace' (cited in Schiff and Ya'ari 1989: 232).

In an early Hamas handbill, it was mentioned that the Israeli Intelligence Service, the Shin Bet, was trying to trap agents with the aid of hashish and other drugs and that it caught young women in its net by having 'stray dogs' (Palestinian collaborators) seduce them. The leaflet said that young girls were being encouraged to frequent hairdressers, boutiques (places young educated women used to run as their private businesses), or even shoe stores without a chaperone (Schiff and Ya'ari 1989: 231). These tactics became known as the Israeli *'isqat'*[11] policy. In response, young men were warned off alcohol, pornographic magazines, and loose women who tried to flirt with them in the street. Thus, strict moral conduct, piety and modesty were elevated to important tools for national resistance and weapons of the underground. According to two Israeli writers: 'Just as the PLO had to grapple with the problem of its permeation by Israeli agents, so Sheikh Yassine's aides looked for ways to prevent penetrations by double agents and to keep new recruits from falling under the Israelis' sway. A prisoner was best off telling his interrogators from the start that he was privy to secret information but would die under torture rather than reveal it' (Schiff and Ya'ari 1989: 232).

Religion in itself has proved a source of great strength in the contest with the Shin Bet, and the Hamas people have been described as 'exceedingly tough nuts to crack' (Schiff and Ya'ari 1989: 230).

This Islamist 'national security policy' has had serious implications for the social order, greatly restricting women's mobility and putting more social pressure on women making 'suspicious' moves. The ways women talk, walk and act have all come under close social scrutiny. In a survey on living conditions in Palestinian society, 56% of women surveyed in

Gaza and 47% in the West Bank said that they were unable to move freely within their communities (Heiberg *et al.* 1993: 306–307). Another consequence of this policy was the crackdown by the movement on some collaborators, drug dealers and prostitutes. Fateh, in its rivalry with the Islamists, felt it had to take the 'lead' in this policy of 'purification' of society, and actively participated in veiling women in Gaza. According to Na'ima (the head of the Fateh women's organisation in Gaza, who herself took up the veil): 'I cannot tell who is Fateh and who is Hamas in harassing women to "urge" them to veil, but I can tell you that our own male members in Fateh were pressuring us in the organisation to veil, they used to tell us Hamas people are not more "moral" than we are' (Naima el-Sheikh, Interview).

Fateh also took the lead in killing more 'loose women'. Between 1988 and 1993, 107 women were killed, 81 of them in Gaza (Be'er and Abdel-Jawad 1994: 89–90). These women had been 'morally suspect', rather than confirmed collaborators. The military organisation of the Islamists was not the main perpetrator of these crimes; Fateh groups came first, followed by groups related to Fateh, and then groups affiliated to the Popular Front (the Marxist Left). These 'morally suspect' women were seen as betraying the honour, not only of their families, but also of their nation; and their elimination became a 'national duty'. Thus, the imperative of upholding the moral order, when facing the colonising power, did not differ much between religious national movements such as Hamas and the secular nationalist groups.

The 'security policy', however, does not fully explain the insistence on veiling as a moral code for women. It is also possible to see it as a tool in the Islamist rivalry with secularist 'non-veiled' groups. Veiling is a unifying cultural marker for the movement and a signifier of its growing strength among Hamas followers. Alternatively, as Keddie suggests, it may be more of a way of asserting communal identity, rather than being such a strong religious marker (Keddie 1998). Veiling can also become an important political symbol employed to forge a new social 'modern' identity, and it can act as a tool in opening new possibilities for women within and outside the movement. Nor should veiling be seen as the only marker of Hamas' gender ideology. Rather, their ideology changes as the power of Islamist women evolves within their movement.

In 1988, Hamas published its *mythaq* (Charter) in which its 'formal' position on gender was spelt out in articles 17 and 18. Article 17 states that 'Muslim women have a role in the liberation struggle that is no less important than the role of men: woman is the maker of men, and her role in guiding and educating the generations is a major role' (Hamas Charter n.d: n.p). In the same article, women were viewed as passive targets for the '"Masons", "Rotary Clubs", intelligence networks – all centres of destruction and saboteurs... And the Islamists should play their role in confronting the schemes of those saboteurs i.e. protecting them' (Hamas Charter, article 17).

In article 18, it was stressed again that 'the woman in the house of the *Mujahed* and the striving family, be she a mother or a sister, has the most important role in caring for the home and raising the children with the ethical character and understanding that comes from Islam' (Hamas Charter, article 18). Women were advised to be economical, to avoid carefree spending and to 'keep in mind that money is blood that must flow only in the veins to sustain the life of children and parents equally'. Women were thus advised to 'give' to their family and nation instead of 'taking', a notion Hamas stresses to differentiate Islamist women from the secular activists. In this vision, women are portrayed as dependent on men, confined to their homes and segregated from public space. However, the vision did not match the reality of what Islamist women and female students were actively 'doing' in the student blocs of Hamas or in Islamist associations. Through their own involvement in the movement, these women were able to alter the vision to make a space for themselves.

The ever evolving gender vision: 'the text does not prohibit'

The observation that 'the text does not prohibit' is a theme that kept recurring throughout my interviews with Amira, Maysoon, Samira and many other women militants. What they meant was that religious texts are open-ended, making it possible to forge for women a wider legitimate space in the public arenas. The daily reality of life for women eager for work, education and political participation shaped a gradual and growing critique inside the movement. Islamist women, while fully complicit in disseminating the movement's gender ideology, are, however, also the first to push its boundaries and stretch their public space.

These evolutions accompanied a change in Hamas strategy after the 'peace process' began and Hamas moved from being a military underground organisation to a political party. During this development, the Salvation Party started to pay more systematic attention to recruiting women, in order to widen its popular base. As the Salvation Party, like other national and secular organisations, began to emphasise the legal political struggle, it became difficult to ignore the conditions in which women lived and to prevent them from joining political life. At the same time, the movement was in full gear, attacking the claims for women's rights by other nationalist and secularist women's organisations. Thus, one can say that there were both internal and external factors pressuring Hamas to deal with women's issues, the latter coming from feminists' demands and the equal rights discourse, which offered a serious challenge to Islamist ideology.

What, then, are women's rights from an Islamic perspective? Here the answer will not come from the male leadership of the party but rather from its women. I am drawing here on the contributions of a workshop and three conferences organised by women activists in Gaza. Papers presented at these conferences clearly illustrate the shift that has been taking place in Islamist women's positions and priorities, as well as in their daily practices and in their experiences within the Party.

The first conference concentrated on de-legitimising other women's groups in order to present Islamist women themselves as the 'true' and 'authentic' voice for women's interests. In the second conference we find an admission that the Islamists have no vision or agenda for women's issues, but at the same time an attempt is made to reinterpret religious texts in order to allow a new reading incorporating what women have achieved so far in society due to modernisation processes. It is astonishing to note that in the process of formulating a new reading for religious texts, a parallel process of 'de-Islamising' the discourse on women's rights took place. At this point, Islamists adopted new terms (such as 'sustainable development'), which up to then had been used predominantly by donors and by feminist activists. By the time we get to the third conference, the concept of sustainable development is itself brought under scrutiny and the applicability of the concept to Palestinian society is questioned. Also, for the first time, a 'modern' and this time 'feminist' critique of the liberal rights approach was used. These conferences were landmarks in the passage of Hamas gender ideology from utter rejection of feminism to borrowing and selectively incorporating positions advocated by feminists. This resulted in a reconceptualisation of the terminology by the Islamists (i.e. they were Islamised), while at the same time, Islamic discourse was de-Islamised and considered within the contemporary framework.

From rejection to engagement

The Women's Department (*daerat al-'amal al-nissaei*) of the Islamic Salvation Party proved energetic in pushing the boundaries of the Islamist women's space within the Party structure and in society at large. On 24 April 1997, a first booklet was published by the Department as an outcome of a one-day workshop (*youm derassi*) entitled 'Palestinian

Woman...Where Next?' The booklet, for the first time in the Brothers' history in Palestine, fills the gaps of their gender agenda and inverts some of their previous positions. In its introduction, the booklet clearly states that the raison d'être of the whole discussion was that it 'became a preoccupying issue for those many who are keen to see women occupying a distinguished position in the society side by side with men' (WAD – Women's Action Department 1997: 1). The booklet asserts that the:

> waves that have surfaced in our society lately all claim to uplift women, as they see fit, but women, who stand on their rights in Islam do not accept these claims. We as Muslim sisters, aware of our great religion, have to stand up strongly and courageously to clarify and spread our thoughts in our advancing society. We are the preachers for the true uplifting *'nahda'* for women through the true, deep and correct understanding of our religion. This will be the true victory for women. (WAD – Women's Action Department 1997: 1)

Many papers (both men's and women's) were presented throughout the April workshop by prominent cultural leaders in Hamas in a systematic attempt to delegitimise the non-Islamic women's groups. They did this by linking women's NGOs to the West, depicting them as a ploy of the West to weaken the nation and betray it by 'smothering' Israel's existence in the heart of the *umma*. It rejected the call for a gender agenda as unfit when the national agenda was at the fore. In the first paper delivered by a prominent cultural and political analyst from *al-Rissala* (*The Message*, a weekly Islamist journal), the speaker Nehad Khalil quoted a leftist activist and writer to show his scepticism about the motives and 'the foreign funding' of the different NGOs advocating rights in Palestinian society. He linked the mushrooming of these groups to the West's desire to create a political environment accepting Israel and to the need of some Palestinian party cadres for jobs and money or personal 'enrichment, through funding, and fame' (Khalil 1997: 3, 4). He added that the motive behind the activism of these organisations was to divert attention towards new issues which 'don't fit with the existing social and economic structures' (Khalil 1997: 4). He rejected recourse to international conventions, a move he said was 'understandable when we talk about human rights violations by the Israelis' to gain international support; 'but, when we dialogue internally as Palestinians about liberties and women we have to start from our culture, heritage and our daily reality' (Khalil 1997: 5).

In my interviews, many Islamist women expressed the same scepticism vis-à-vis universal rights for women. Maysoon, for example, states:

> Isn't it weird to hear the same discourse all over the Arab world and the Islamic world by many women's organisations. How come all women's needs and aspirations are the same all over a spectrum of different societies with different contexts and needs? Where is the specificity of each society, where are the variations between them and among women themselves? This is a standard blueprint strategy pushed not by women but by foreign donors. (Maysoon, Interview)

However, the workshop of April 1997 could not reject outright the prevailing discourse on women's rights. There were nuances among activists claiming women's rights. Some feminists called for the prohibition of polygamy and the right to divorce within *shari'a* law; others called for restrictions on polygamy without outright prohibition.

After rejecting feminists' calls, Nehad Khalil scorned the position of the PA:

> The Authority has no special agenda for women. It adopts neither a liberal vision, nor a conservative one, let alone a religious one. The PA is keen to talk about women's rights and equality superficially, as window dressing. This is mainly to give the impression to the world that our society is modern and respects women and their rights. This lack of agenda is reflected in the contradictory behaviours of the PA. While we have a woman minister and a woman ambassador in the PA, the Ministry of Interior issued a rule to ask women to get the consent of their guardians to issue their passports. (Khalil 1997: 7)

Finally, Khalil acknowledged that, after asserting that 'Islam dignified women and gave them their rights', Islamists paid little attention to women's interests once the struggle against the Occupation came. In this, he said, the Islamists were like the nationalists before them. All the same, Islamists could not ignore the issues; as Khalil said: 'the issue is on the table now, there is a debate about family law and its reform, on early marriage and its prohibition… etc' (Khalil 1997: 7).

I would treat this paper as an admission by an Islamist that de-legitimising 'others' is no longer a viable practice. Most importantly, the paper raises the need to know what women's actual situations are. This call was reflected in the recommendations of the paper, which included giving more attention to studies, in particular to those of women in Islamist circles. There was an appeal not only to establish a study centre but also to direct more attention by intellectuals and researchers towards laws, ideas, visions and studies proposed by secularist women (Khalil 1997: 8).

A paper presented by Khitam Abu Musa inverted the gender vision of the Hamas Charter of 1988. In her paper, she interprets Islam as the religion that gave woman all her rights: education, free choice of a husband, inheritance (widely denied by custom), mobility (to participate in the call for the rule of God and *jihad*), proselytising, and social or professional work (Abu Musa 1997: 17–21). By stressing a more controversial issue – that of 'mixing with men' – the paper concludes, 'thus, now we can see that Muslim woman was moved to prove herself in all aspects and fields of life. Islam allows women to meet men (*'abah'*), and to exchange dialogue if she is committed to the *'adab shar'eia* (the conventions of *shari'a*)' (Abu Musa 1997: 21). According to Amira Haroun, this is to be understood within the framework of a woman's adopting Islamic dress and maintaining respectable manners in line with religious customs.

In her interpretation of religion and *shari'a*, Khitam Abu Musa cities the authority of religious text to emphasise that 'the urge of women to develop (*intilaq*, i.e. to flourish) and participate in social life with all that entails, including meeting men, is an approach *decided* [emphasis added] by the Islamic *shari'a* and prophet's *sunna* (deeds)' (Abu Musa 1997: 17–21). She also addresses the concept of 'public good', stressing that 'Islam *mandates* [emphasis added] women to go out and participate in social life because the opening up of public work for women is for the good (*al-khayr*) of the spread of a serious, beneficial life for more Muslims. This begins with a request for the provision of education and entails aiding a husband in earning a living and participating in beneficial social work or political activism that supports goodness and fights the trivial' (Abu Musa 1997: 22).

The vision presented by this speaker is not shared by all Islamist women in the Party; it seems more pertinent to the needs of educated women who want to abolish the sex segregation code in order to benefit from more opportunities in the labour market. Women with less education don't share this view: 'in the Party they are irritated when we insist on being separate. The Party says that as a developmental party there is no harm in mixing, but this is against our traditions' (Fatmeh, Interview). Some Party cadres and educated women are more open to changes than some of their grassroots constituencies.

As Islamists attempted to 'purify' their new stand, separating it from past involvement in 'backwardness', they found it important to detach Islam from the oppression of women and to claim that such negative behaviours were due to 'Palestinian mentality' and 'backwardness'. The older ways, they said, represented 'ignorance and limited vision characterised by sharp contradictions and imbalances, while the new way recognizes women's value and assigns them ethical and moral status' (Salah Bardaweel, editor-in-chief of *The Message* [*al-Rissala*]; Bardaweel 1997: 28). Bardaweel claims that the latter viewpoint is 'less known due to the underdeveloped phases which Palestinian society went through', but says that that study of Islamic revivals during different periods in Islamic history shows that Islamic leaders 'gave woman more attention by providing for her education, culture (*tathkifiha*), and the development of her capacities in her house, society and nation' (Bardaweel 1997: 28).

A booklet documenting the proceedings of the April workshop included a section on women in international conventions and in 1995 Beijing conference resolutions, as well as recommendations for the Party. The recommendations included some interesting points on 'dissemination and advocacy' of women's issues within the Party. Also recommended were: formation of Palestinian feminist *nassawi* (cadres) through debates and Islamic workshops; a study of contemporary universal conventions from a comparative perspective; embodiment of women's rights in practice; and formulation of an education programme for men, to help them become more sensitive to women's roles (WAD – Women's Action Department 1997: 44).

Mahmoud al-Zahar, a prominent leader in Hamas, argues in a paper he presented at the 1999 women's conference that women in Islam have equal rights to men in all aspects of work. He adds, however, that women's labour must differ in two cases: when the work might lead to a contradiction in *shari'a* and when the work might not be suitable for women's capabilities and characteristics (*qodorateha and khossosseyateha*) – but he does not specify what these characteristics are (Al-Zahar 1999: 4). In the same paper, al-Zahar offers a brilliant formulation of the concepts of the 'public' and 'private' domains around a controversial issue relating to men's dominance (*qewama*) in the family – a formulation that flagrantly contradicts the notion of equality advocated by feminists, since it puts women under men's authority. Al-Zahar interprets men's supremacy in terms of the economic and managerial, rather than in political terms. He states that '*qewama* does not mean absolute authority, but means that a man takes the responsibility to provide for the material and emotional needs of the family, to provide protection, care and administer (*yassos*) the family according to principles of justice' (Al-Zahar 1999: 4). Al-Zahhar links *qewama* with another principle which he sees as applicable not only to the public sphere, or polity, but also to the private sphere. This is the principle of *al-shoura* (consultation or deliberation). As he puts it: 'Muslims should understand that *al-shoura* and *al-qewama* are not conditions of tyranny or despotism (*halat istebdad*), but are phenomena in which all members of the family participate in their own way (*shorakaa*) as part of family management. Like the state, the family can only be built on *shoura*' (Al-Zahar 1999: 4).

Al-Zahar sees authoritarianism in the family as a sort of extremism (*tatarof*), the loss of *qewama* as chaos (*ifrat*) and both as reasons for the collapse of family, society and state. Therefore, democratisation à la Islamism is not only a concern in the public sphere but is also very relevant to the private sphere – to the relationships between husband and wife as well as between parents and children. This 'new' interpretation was voiced by one of my interviewees. In Maysoon's words:

> In my family, we are used to discussing and deliberating our daily plan. I encourage my children to choose what they want to eat, to wear, to do, and to study, and of course, we allow my girl to choose who she wants to marry. But the man she wants has to come in the open to ask for her hand and not to meet her secretly. Once everything is in the open, we facilitate all the steps. Our religion is *yosser* (easy going) and not *'ossr* (hard to follow). (Maysoon, Interview)

Maysoon refers not only to daily democratic participation in her family but also to what has become a common trend among Islamists facilitating marriage arrangements for young couples. The new arrangements endeavour to minimise marriage expenses and to refrain from 'unnecessary' and extravagant expenditures (wedding parties in hotels, big meals, flowers, etc). They reduce the dowry and gold presents a bride should have.

At the women's conferences held by the Women's Action Department in 1999 and 2000, many other papers were presented that tried to formulate a more progressive gender vision stemming from *al-shari'a*. However, while the starting point was the 'text', the call for new interpretations was always linked to the needs of society and the 'spirit of the age' (*roh al-'assr*).[12] Religious discourse was gradually distanced from a more 'modern' and temporal discourse. The usual empty, repetitive religious discourse vis-à-vis other women's groups was criticised as a 'traditional' Islamic discourse. One paper articulated a well-grounded knowledge of development discourse in Palestine, and in particular of the sustainable development approach. The writer, Nehad al-Sheikh Khalil, attributed the failure of development efforts in Palestinian society to the lack of full use of women's capacities. He cited the need to reform all legislation, especially family law, and to transform values and customs that discriminate against women. He advocated providing women with better health care and family planning, noting that early marriage and high fertility reduce women to the reproductive role. He raised the issue of women's dependency on men, pointing out that it enhances their subordination.

In his diagnosis, the speaker used an alternative discourse based not on the 'religious text' but on a different interpretation development, involving secular notions of public good and national interest. He focused not on the 'Islamicness' (cultural specificity) of Muslim societies but on the specificity of living under Occupation. Thus, although 'reducing fertility will weaken our demographic strength against our enemies ... this should not be at the expense of women's health' (Khalil 1999: 4). Focusing on women's individual rights 'in isolation from their families and children is dangerous', he asserted, 'since we have not yet any alternative institutions to care for them ... Work at home does not reduce women's status, and it should be valued, morally ... Women's role in society needs her education and her openness to society and her participation' (Khalil 1999: 5, 6).

In criticising feminist calls for women's rights based on the notion of individual rights, he stated that 'the individual self cannot be the measure for development, since this might contradict the public good of the society' (Khalil 1999: 6). An example, he suggested, would be a Palestinian working in an Israeli settlement or workshop. Such a person, he said, 'can gain a lot individually, but this will be at the expense of our agricultural land (on which the settlements are built) and our economy' (Khalil 1999: 6). He added that 'in strong Western economies, the individual can be the focus of development, but not in our case where we are under Occupation and suffer from a lack of democracy. Our context necessitates the collective mobilisation of people in order to resist the Occupation; [we are in] a phase of giving to the nation and not yet taking from it' (Khalil 1999: 6).

This paper manifested awareness of the global debate on the causes of underdevelopment and their relationship to internal factors (i.e. lack of democratisation and lack of good governance), as well as to external factors (i.e. unequal North–South relations) (Tornquist 1999). But Khalil's paper warned that the call for democracy and women's liberation was being used as 'an ideological weapon by neo-colonisers in the age of globalisation, to convince subjugated peoples that their defeats were related to their lack of democracy and their women's status and not to the coloniser's exploitation and the drain of their wealth'. In the Palestinian context, the speaker asserted, issues of democracy and women's rights are wielded to 'disintegrate our Palestinian social structure which always reproduces resistance, refuses Occupation, and refuses to normalise relations with our enemies' (Khalil 1999: 6).

The new reading of sustainable development discourse by Islamists will create more difficulties for secularists and nationalists in general, and for nationalist and secularist women's movements in particular. The latter, due to the national struggle, have not taken a clear position on issues related to women's fertility or the philosophy behind the call for sustainable development. This lack of clarity, one can predict, will give more ammunition to articulate Islamist discourse.

At the second and third women's conferences in 1999 and 2000, a rather more 'secure' and less defensive approach was adopted in addition to a more rational position vis-à-vis international conventions. The total de-legitimisation of the 'other', in particular other feminist women's organisations, was changed in favour of more engagement. The 1999 conference postulated a distinction between organisations working in good faith as different national actors and their donors, who 'are not innocent and who work according to their own agendas' (Documents of the Second Women's Conference 1999). Criticising the total rejection manifested in the workshop of 1997, this conference expressed agreement that 'our approach to women's liberation is Islam and not the universal conventions; however, we don't reject any of these conventions as long as they don't contradict the rules of Islamic *shari'a* and the specificity of the Palestinian Muslim society' (Documents of the Second Women's Conference 1999).

The conclusions of these conferences can be encapsulated in two main points. First, Islamists should change. They should anticipate Islamic reform and take the lead in the uplifting (*nahda*) of women; otherwise, 'others' will lead. Second, emphasis should be placed on the idea that 'the mission to liberate women and activate their role falls primarily on women. Women have to claim their rights and struggle for them in the light of the proper understanding of the tolerant *shari'a*'.

The third conference, in 2000, was dedicated to outlining more specifically the differences that exist between *shari'a* and international conventions. From this conference emerged a more thoughtful critique of women's rights discourse as it figures in the international conventions. For the first time, papers presented and questioned, not the viability of rights discourse altogether, but its liberal, utilitarian individualistic western basis and in their critiques, employed critical feminist thinking (Phillips 1993). In Amira Haroun's paper, for example, we read: 'The concept of rights was established (in the West) on utilitarianism, thus, utilitarian individualism supersedes rationality and engulfs all social relations ... this conception is false since the individual was never an abstract being; the individual was always a social being' (Haroun 2000: 1).

Thus, the discourse of the women's NGOs, based on liberal individual rights, was contested by another 'western', 'feminist' discourse based on the notion of active citizenship[13] used this time by Islamist women. Islamist critiques of liberalism, like socialist feminist ones, question the morality of narrowly defending the principle of individual rights and of allowing this to take precedence over the question of social responsibility. Citizenship is usually conceived of as an individual right alone, and in political terms is reduced to the limited practice of voting, reflecting an impoverished view of social membership. Instead, some argue that there is a need for a more substantive version that is based on participation and social responsibility known as social citizenship (Molyneux 1996: 260). We read again in Haroun's paper that 'in our Islamic vision, the notion of the individual is seen in its relation to the collective. That is why the notion of individual rights in Islam is formed in the context of duties which help to awake in the individual the incentives to "give" and not only to "take"' (Haroun 2000: 5).

The emphasis in Islamic discourse on this 'give-and-take' approach is linked to the 'specific' situation of the Palestinian people, which they argue is not cultural, but rather national, occurring at a particular historical conjuncture. This is a dimension that is very much missing in feminist NGO discourse. The emphasis on 'giving to the nation' should be seen in the context of a matter missing in the national agenda being offered by secular, feminist women's movements in Palestine. It should also be seen in a context in which the first audible women's voice in Palestine was the feminist voice, claiming rights and obfuscating what should be given to the nation under the continuing Occupation.

Thus, in the absence of a clear national agenda drawn by the nationalist, secularist women's movement, Islamists link women's rights with the national and social needs of the Palestinian people, asking women, as did the old nationalist discourse, to serve the nation, à la Islamism this time, and to reproduce more men (Anthias and Yuval-Davis 1989).

From words to deeds

Islamist women have managed to build impressive, well-organised women's constituencies among highly educated and professional women, at times using more temporal discourses based on sustainable development and women's rights, as well as on new interpretations of religious texts. The question arises as to how these new readings are reflected in daily practices within the Party. I highlight here an increasing tendency to foster gender equality, not merely complementarity, and more egalitarian social ideals.

The efforts of the Women's Action Department in the Salvation Party opened a space for common ground between men and women by 'mainstreaming' gender issues into the dominant politics of an Islamic party. The success of the Department in effecting this important change within the Islamic movement went hand in hand with demands for equal pay. In criticising the Party for privileging men's work over women's, the Department was persistent in calling for equal job opportunities and pay for men and women doing the same work. The two female members of the politburo[14] recall:

> In our work with women, we need more people. We started to demand the hiring of more women; they accepted reluctantly, but for half the pay.[15] They [the male members] thought that women didn't have the same responsibilities as men, but we refused – how did they know that women have not the same responsibilities? – it is a question of principle – if women do the same work as men, they have to get the same payment ... we managed to put an equal number of *motafareghat* [full-time paid women members] in the regional administrative committees before the closure of the Party local branches; and we were also heading towards having the same number of paid women as men in our journal office before its closure by the PA. (Youssra and Amira, Interview)

The Department's call for equal treatment by the Party reaches inside the home. Here, the Department eschews the 'rights discourse' of feminists in favour of a more pragmatic strategy of 'looking for solutions'. In Amira's words:

> Everybody in the Party claims that he supports woman's work, woman's development, but they don't put effort into supporting her in her work. If they want her to succeed, inside and outside, then the men have to support her in the *home* [emphasis added] in order to succeed in society. In this respect, we avoid talking about what men 'have' to do but we try to '*involve*' [emphasis added] them in finding solutions such as supporting her at home, establishing a nursery and kindergarten close to her house. In this respect, we fully support the call of the Women's Affairs Committee[16] in their demand for an hour for working mothers to breast feed their babies, but this also requires nurseries in each workplace for women. (Amira, Interview)

Inside the Party, women leaders rejected the assertion by Hamas leader al-Zahhar that their work should be 'suitable for women's capabilities and characteristics'. They called for total equality in two respects: in their daily work in the Party and in their rejection of the claim that women are not equal to men in military activities. On the issue of daily work, the Islamist women in the Party stated:

> In the daily work we have so many activities. One of the most successful events we organise each year is the political prisoners' exhibition in which we establish a big tent to host all sorts of activities: exhibiting their paintings and belongings, displaying their pictures and writings... etc. To build the tent we used to ask the help of our men; this happened only in the first year. When we started to push for hiring more women with equal pay, we decided to build the tent ourselves. We wanted to show them that we are not less powerful and if we want we can do exactly what they do. Now, each year, we build the tent from A to Z by ourselves. (Youssra and Amira, Interview)

It is worth noting here, that the two leaders' approach not only contradicts that of some Islamist men but also that of some Islamist women. Maysoon and Samira, Islamist women's leaders in the West Bank, assert that they don't share this vision, viewing women's roles as complementary, rather than equal, to that of men. The case of *istishhadeyyat* (female conscious martyrs) is another example, and highlights the involvement of women in military activities. This suggests that there are differences not only between Islamist men and women but among the women themselves.

Shari'a politics and a possible common ground

I have argued throughout that it is the political context rather than the religious text that determines Islamist discourse. The 'modified', ever-evolving version of *shari'a* displayed by Hamas raises two issues. On the one hand, it is a challenge to the discourse used by feminist NGOs – a discourse based on a liberal, individualistic notion of rights and one that ignores the plight the nation faces under Occupation. By putting Islam at the centre of a modified notion of Palestinian nationalism, the Islamists have managed to de-legitimise feminist women's discourse, portraying it as non-national and alien. On the other hand, the Islamist position also poses a challenge to the rather ambivalent Palestinian secularism that used Islam as a source of its legitimacy. By 'Islamising' Palestine and 'nationalising' Islam, the Islamists have proved successful in forging a brand of nationalism in which Islam was integral and which constituted a mobilising force for the masses.

In such a context, secularists, while pressuring and challenging the Islamists, are nonetheless losing ground by advocating a discourse of rights in isolation from the national agenda and in the absence of a mobilising organisation. NGO activism, based on short-lived projects, does not have the potential to constitute an alternative. By becoming an opposition movement setting itself against all forms of violation of civic and human rights, Islamists have developed a political organisation. In contrast, women working in NGOs have no organised constituency; and the support they do have, when they get it, is derived from a decaying de-legitimised authority.

In the analysis presented above, I showed how Islamist women forged a space for a category of educated women from poor, mainly refugee backgrounds, in which it was morally correct to be active in all spheres of public life. I also showed how they managed to establish themselves among other poor women by providing services for them and defending the rights of male prisoners. This is an important accomplishment for women's activism in a phase of national struggle.

However, in the above analysis I highlighted two different instances in which *shari'a*, as a guiding principle for women's rights, was used in contradictory ways. In the debate provoked by feminist women's organisations, *shari'a* was used first by Islamists as a fixed, divine and immutable idiom to de-legitimise and to silence the non-Islamic women's groups. At the same time, it was used to discredit the PA's advocacy of the notion of popular sovereignty as the basis for new legislation. It is still uncertain whether Islamists want instead to establish a sovereignty belonging to God, since their state project has yet to be spelt out.

The same debate on *shari'a* triggered debate within the Islamic movement itself. Islamists' search for an alternative to the secular feminist platform ironically brought them into continuous engagement with it. I showed that highly educated and professional Islamist women employed in their discourse the total equality approach to defend equal rights for women in the public sphere (at least in work and political activism) and in their daily practice.

I also showed how the top male leadership reacted swiftly to 'fix' the *shari'a* (Zubaida 2003: 1) in another set of laws concerning the Penal Code, again to silence and discourage feminist and secularist women's groups from suggesting any reforms. The fact that the top male leadership put its full weight behind *shari'a* is significant not only for women's rights;

it is also an assertion of hegemonic power for Islamists in society generally and vis-à-vis the PA. It may also indicate the still uncertain nature of any future Palestinian or Islamic state through a strategy of active citizenship.

In this respect, Molyneux warns, 'social citizenship understood as community activism, participation, or moral regeneration is not always or indeed necessarily linked to projects for democratic reform or greater social cohesion. In some countries it is manipulated by 'fundamentalists' who seek to create a political community, in the furtherance of objectives that would lead to authoritarian, theocratic and highly gendered states' (Molyneux 1996: 260). This will not necessarily happen. My data show that Islamists, in their quest for a platform as a national movement, were obliged to borrow and incorporate new visions in order to be inclusive such as pluralism, women's rights, the public good, sustainable development, the social self versus the individual self, all borrowed and co-opted by the Islamists from the secular context. The evidence shows that certain arenas of civil society activism, such as the student movement, included women militants in a positive way, and that the Party structure itself incorporated women who were sociologically marginalised from the national leadership, in which women of the elite were over-represented.

However, while there are moments of opening and engagement, there are also many contradictions that might lead to closure and to a retreat into interpretations of Islam that would affect women negatively. Islamists could return to an insistence on the role of women solely as reproducers of the nation. Their stand on polygamy is not yet clear. There has been heated debate on the 'suitability' of women for military actions, but what sort of 'Islamic' state this activism might lead to depends, to a great extent, on the general context set by secularists.

Islamist women's discourse does not stem only from the Quran but also from positive engagement with discourses of other groups, whether secular feminists or nationalists. In my opinion, this engagement provides the impulse for Islamist women to go back to the religious text and to look for possible new readings, in order to respond to the challenges posed by other women's groups. The interaction between the different perspectives could lead to a realisation that they share a common ground: Islamists could unite with secularist and nationalist women in pushing for new readings of religious texts, as well as engage in the daily realities of women who are facing the daily oppression of the Israeli occupation in the context of the unsolved national struggle. This mutual accommodation on the basis of the national agenda (Norton 1993; Hudson 1996; Salame 2001) requires each party to maintain vigilance with regard to the changes occurring in the approaches and discourses of the other instead of adopting an approach of total rejection, which has been taken by women's NGOs.

Islamists have had to build on women's modern gains in areas such as education and work opportunities. This suggests that the nature of the state they might claim will not depend on a religious blueprint, but will depend to a great extent on what form of state and society they live in and on the visions and challenges posed by other nationalist and secularist groups if these groups are sufficiently supported by a substantial majority and power. Finally, the claim that the ongoing conflict between the two rival parties Hamas and Fateh is a struggle between the 'forces of darkness' and the 'modernising forces' has no empirical foundation. This discourse is used to cover up the real differences over the national agenda and over the best strategies to adopt in order to achieve the Palestinian national goals of self-determination and liberation.

Notes

1. Bassam Jarrar, one of the outspoken leaders in Hamas, has hurled this accusation at feminists, maintaining publications, for example, feminists were depicted as part of 'a secular, feminist octopus which seeks to strangle the body of our ruined homeland' (Al-Huda Association 1998: 3).

2. Scholars such as Lawrence (1987), Munson (1988), Binder (1988) and Baron (1996) hold to the use of the term 'fundamentalism'. Since the early 1980s, a growing number of scholars have objected to this term in relation to modern Islamic movements and their ideologies. Critics have drawn attention to four defects that accompany its use: taxonomic error, taxonomic imprecision, polemical distortion and ideological mobilisation (Esposito 1992: 7; Campo 1995: 172). Nikki Keddie uses the term 'religionpolitical' instead of 'fundamentalist' to describe the movement (Keddie 1999: 11–12).
3. It is also worth noting that Fateh also used to call a woman member *ukhot* (sister) while in the leftist parties she is called *rafiqa* (comrade).
4. The same could be said about women's representation in the leadership of the secular political parties, which is relatively low despite the impressive activism of many women's organisations. Women are sharply underrepresented in the Central Committees of the political parties: they comprise 10% of the Central Committee of the Popular Front for the Liberation of Palestine, nearly 19% of Fida's, 19.5% of the Democratic Front for the Liberation of Palestine and only 5% in the Central Committee of Fateh (Sida 1999: 21).
5. In 2001, the PA raided local Party offices to confiscate all its equipment, documents and computers and issued a rule to ban it from all activities as well as the banning of its journal *'al-Rissala'*. According to Amira, the Party functions at a very low level only from its headquarters in Gaza city. At this moment, even though the Party managed to obtain a ruling on 21 March 2003 from the Highest Court cancelling the PA ruling no. 113/2003, which allowed the PA to put its hand on the budgets of 39 Islamic societies, the PA refuses to implement the ruling and renewed its own budget-taking powers with ruling no. 40/ 2004; Palestine Information Centre (www.Palestine-info.net).
6. The usual presence of political leaders is that of attending the inaugurations of women's conferences for some time and then leaving, but without presenting theoretical papers which show more involvement in the event. The content of the paper will be dealt with in a separate part.
7. www.Palestine-info.net, accessed 16 July 2003.
8. Bourdieu distinguishes between doxa and orthodoxy. Doxa is when there is a quasi-perfect correspondence between the objective order and the subjective principles of organisation (as in ancient societies), the natural and social worlds appear as self-evident. This distinguishes it from the orthodox and heterodox, which imply the awareness and recognition of the possibility of different or antagonistic beliefs (Eagleton and Bourdieu 1992: 111–121).
9. This policy was to be changed later after the crackdown on Hamas in 1989 and 1990 by the Israeli forces with its concomitant practices of severe torture on Hamas members. In 1990, when Izz el-Dinn el-Qassam was established as the military wing of Hamas and after its members experienced much Israeli torture, it was realised that 'the talk about the utmost internal strength and empowerment was demystified by the reality on the ground, very few people proved able to sustain the violent physical and psychological torture while the majority collapsed. The new policy was if a member goes for military operations he should realise his target and withdraw safely or resist to the end if he was encircled with no surrender as an option' (Abul-Omrein 2000: 353). This might be the background for the suicide bombers rather than the 'death culture' propagated by the Israeli and western media.
10. There are some contradictory accounts on the exact year of these organisations, some give 1982, others give 1984 or 1985 (see Abul-Omrein 2000: 196–197).
11. *Isqat* in Arabic could have many meanings: 'fall down in a trap' or lowering someone to collaboration, the term could denote the sexual corruption or moral corruption in the case of collaborators, but in the Palestinian context, it denotes the methods used by the Israelis to use or seduce the victim and force them to work against their people's national interests.
12. Papers presented to the second conference on the Palestinian Woman 'Between the Actual Challenges and the Future Aspirations' on 16 August 1999, in particular those of Lamia Abu Jalala and Nehad Khalil.
13. The recent debate on women's rights and citizenship found its way into the Islamist women's discourse. The Islamist thinkers (Tamimi 2002; ElMessiri 2003) follow the critiques of the Enlightenment principles of universality and individualism offered by Marxist feminists and postmodernists. These critiques suggest that, if citizenship could be re-fashioned in a way that divested it from abstract universalism and 'false egalitarianism', it could be a more effective tool in advancing gender justice. Some authors have claimed that sex difference and the female body should be the proper basis of legal and political recognition (Phillips 1993; Lister 1997; Voet 1998).
14. In 2000 they were Youssra and Amira. In the third round of elections in 2001, Amira was elected again and Fatemah Saleh replaced Youssra.
15. It is common in Gaza, where the unemployment rate is very high (39%), to pay women less than men in private business and in general women are less well paid (81.3% of male wages in Gaza and 66% in the West Bank) (Sida 1999: 26–27).
16. A secular, feminist women's coalition.

References

Abu Musa, Khitam (1997) 'Women in Islamic thought' 'al-marah fil tasawour al-islami'. Paper presented at the workshop 'Palestinian Woman. Where Next?' ('al-marah al-falestineyya ila ayna'), Gaza, April.

Abul-Omrein, Khaled (2000) *Hamas: The Islamic Resistance Movement in Palestine* (*Hamas: harakat al-moqawameh al-islameyya fi falastine*), Cairo: Marqaz al-Hadara al-'Arabeyya (The Arab Civilisation Centre).

Al-Azmeh, Aziz (1996) *Islams and Modernities*, 2nd edn, London and New York: Verson.

Al-Huda Association (1998) *Palestinian Woman and the Plot of Secular Women* (*al-mara' al-falestenyya wa mo'amrat al-'al-a'maneyyat*), Al Bireh: Al-Huda association.

Al-Messiri, Abdelwahab and Al-Azmeh, Aziz (2000) *Secularism Under Scrutiny* (*Al-'almaniyya taht al-mijhar*), Damascus: Dar al-Fikr al-Mu'asir.

Al-Zahar, Mahmoud (1999) 'Women and political participation' 'al-marah wal mosharaka al-seyasseya'. Paper presented at the Second Women Conference: 'Palestinian Woman between Actual Challenges and Future Aspirations' ('al-marah al-falestineyya bayna tahadeyat al-waqe' wa tomohat al-mostaqbal'), Gaza, 16 August.

Anthias, Floya and Yuval-Davis, Nira (1989) 'Introduction'. In Floya Anthias and Nira Yuval-Davis (eds) *Woman-Nation-State*, Houndmills, Basingstoke, Hampshire and London: Macmillan, 1–15.

Asad, Talal (2003) *Formation of the Secular: Christianity, Islam, Modernity*, Stanford, CA: Stanford University Press.

Badran, Margot (1994) 'Gender activism: feminists and Islamists in Egypt'. In V.M. Moghadam (ed.) *Identity Politics and Women: Cultural Reassertions and Feminisms in International Perspective*, Boulder: Westview Press, 202–227.

Bardaweel, Salah (1997) 'Palestinian woman: to where?' 'al-marah al-falestineyya ila ayna'. Paper presented at the workshop 'Palestinian Woman: to Where?', Gaza, 28 April.

Baron, Beth (1996) 'Silence on attacks on women by fundamentalists', *Contention* 5(3): 99–117.

Be'er, Yizhar and Abdel-Jawad, Saleh (1994) *Collaborators in the Occupied Territories: Human Rights Abuses and Violations*, Jerusalem: B'tselem, the Israeli Information Center for Human Rights in the Occupied Territories.

Binder, Leonard (1988) *Islamic Liberalism: A Critique of Development Ideologies*, Chicago: University of Chicago Press.

Budeiri, Musa (1995) 'The nationalist dimension of Islamic movements in Palestinian politics', *Journal of Palestine Studies* 24(3): 194–208.

Campo, Juan Eduardo (1995) 'The ends of Islamic fundamentalism: hegemonic discourse and the Islamic question in Egypt', *Contention* 4(3): 168–194.

Cohen, Amnon (1982) *Political Parties in the West Bank Under the Jordanian Regime, 1949–1967*, Ithaca, NY: Cornell University Press.

Documents of the Second Women's Conference (1999) 'Closing Statement'. Statement presented at the conference 'Palestinian Woman between Actual Challenges and Future Aspirations' ('al-marah al-falestineyya bayna tahadeyat al-waqe' wa tomohat al-mostaqbal'), Gaza, 16 August.

Eagleton, Terry and Bourdieu, Pierre (1992) 'Pierre, Doxa and common life', *New Left Review* 191: 111–121.

El-Hamad, Jawad and Al Bargothi, Eyad (1997) *A Study in the Political Ideology of the Islamic Resistance Movement, Hamas 1987–1996* (*derassa fi fikr harakat al-moqawamah al-islameyya hamas*), Amman: Middle East Study Centre.

ElMessiri, Abdel-Wahab (2003) 'Towards a new Islamic discourse: re-capturing the Islamic paradigm', www.islamonline.net, accessed 17 July 2003.

Esposito, John L. (1992) *The Islamic Threat: Myth or Reality?*, New York and Oxford: Oxford University Press.

Hammami, Rema (1991) 'Women's political participation in the intifada, a critical overview'. Paper presented at The Intifada and Some Women's Social Issues conference, Jerusalem, 14 December; Ramallah: Women's Studies Committee of Bisan Centre for Research and Development.

Hammami, Rema (1997) *Palestinian Women: A Status Report – Labor and Economy: Gender Segmentation in Palestinian Economic Life*, Palestine: Bir Zeit University, Women's Studies Programme.

Haroun, Amira (2000) 'Introduction'. Paper presented at the Third Women Conference 'Palestinian Woman and Social Change' ('al-marah al-falestineyya wal tahawlat al-ijtema'eyya'), Gaza, 8–9 August.

Hasso, Frances Susan (1997) 'Paradoxes of gender/politics: nationalism, feminism, and modernity in contemporary Palestine', PhD thesis, University of Michigan.

Hawley, John Stratton (1994) *Fundamentalism and Gender*, Oxford and New York: Oxford University Press.

Heiberg, Marianne and Ovensen, Geir (eds) (1993) Palestinian Society. In *Gaza, West Bank and Arab Jerusalem: A Survey of Living Conditions*, Oslo: FAFO, http://www.fafo.no/engelsk/pub/index.htm.

Hobsbawm, Eric (1983) 'Introduction: inventing traditions'. In E. Hosbsbawm and Terence Ranger (eds) *The Invention of Tradition,* Cambridge: Cambridge University Press, 1–14.

Hroub, Khalid (2000) *Hamas Political Thought and Practices,* Washington, DC: Institute of Palestine Studies.

Hudson, Michael (1996) 'Obstacles to democratisation in the Middle East', *Contention* 14: 81–106.

INSP (1995) 'The primary statement of the Islamic national salvation party', 11 December, Gaza, internal party document.

Jad, Islah (1990) 'From salons to the popular committees: Palestinian women, 1919–1989'. In Jamal R. Nassar and Roger Heacock (eds) *Intifada: Palestine at the Crossroads,* New York: Praeger, 125–142.

Jad, Islah (2000) *Palestinian Women: A Status Report – Women and Politics,* Palestine: Bir Zeit University, Women's Studies Institute.

Jad, Islah (2004) 'The "NGOisation" of the Arab women's movement', *IDS Bulletin* 35(4): 27–34.

Kandiyoti, Deniz (1991) 'Identity and its discontents: women and the nation', *Millennium Journal of International Studies* 20(3): 429–443.

Kandiyoti, Deniz (1996) 'Contemporary feminist scholarship and Middle East Studies'. In D. Kandiyoti (ed.) *Gendering the Middle East,* New York: Syracuse University Press, 1–28.

Karam, Azza (1998) *Women, Islamisms and the State: Contemporary Feminisms in Egypt,* London: Macmillan Press; New York: St. Martin's Press.

Keddie, Nikki R. (1998) 'The new religious politics: where, when, and why do "fundamentalisms" appear?', *Comparative Studies in Society and History* 40(4): 696–723.

Keddie, Nikki R. (1999) 'The new religious politics and women worldwide: a comparative study', *Journal of Women's History, Women and Twentieth-Century Religious Politics* 10(4): 11–34.

Khalil, Nehad (1997) 'Status of Palestinian woman in the context of social change' '"waqi" al-marah al-falestineyya fi seyaq al-taghayor al-ijtima'. Paper presented at the workshop 'Palestinian Woman: to Where?' ('al-marah al-falestineyya ila ayn'), Gaza, April.

Khalil, Nehad (1999) 'Women's role in the development process' 'dour al-marah fi 'amaleyat al-tanmeyya'. Paper presented at the Second Women Conference: 'Palestinian Woman between Actual Challenges and Future Aspirations' ('al-marah al-falestineyya bayna tahadeyat al-waqe' wa tomohat al-mostaqbal'), Gaza, 16 August.

Kuttab, Eileen (1993) 'Palestinian women in the intifada: fighting on two fronts', *Arab Studies Quarterly* 15(2): 69–85.

Lawrence, Bruce (1987) 'Muslim fundamentalists movements: reflections toward a new approach'. In Barbara Stowasser (ed.) *The Islamic Impulse,* Washington, DC, London and Sydney: Croom Helm in association with Center for Contemporary Arab Studies, Georgetown University, 15–36.

Lister, Ruth (1997) *Citizenship: Feminist Perspectives,* New York: New York University Press.

Massad, Joseph (1995) 'Conceiving the masculine: gender and Palestinian nationalism', *Middle East Journal* 49(3): 467–483.

Milton-Edwards, Beverley (1996) *Islamic Politics in Palestine,* London: Tauris Academic Studies.

Moghadam, Valentine (1993) 'Islamist movements and women's responses'. In Valentine Moghadam (ed.) *Modernizing Women; Gender and Social Change in the Middle East,* Boulder, CO: Lynne Rienner Publishers, 135–170.

Moghadam, Valentine (1994) 'Introduction: women and identity politics in theoretical and comparative perspective'. In Valentine Moghadam (ed.) *Identity Politics and Women: Cultural Reassertions, Gender and Feminisms in International Perspective,* Boulder, CO: Westview Press, 3–26.

Mohanty, Chandra T. (1991) 'Introduction: cartographies of struggle: Third World women and the politics of feminism'. In C. Mohanty, A. Russo and L. Torres (eds) *Third World Women and the Politics of Feminism,* Indianapolis: Indiana University Press, 1–47.

Molyneux, Maxine (1996) 'Women's rights and the international context in the post-communist states'. In M. Threlfall (ed.) *Mapping the Women's Movement: Feminist Politics and Social Transformation in the North,* London: Verso, 232–260.

Munson, Henry (1988) *Islam and Revolution in the Middle East,* New Haven: Yale University Press.

Norton, Augustus Richard (1993) 'The future of civil society in the Middle East', *The Middle East Journal* 47(2): 205–216.

Papanek, Hanna (1994) 'The ideal woman and the ideal society: control and autonomy in the construction of identity'. In Valentine Moghadam (ed.) *Identity Politics and Women: Cultural Reassertion and Feminisms in International Perspective,* Boulder, CO: Westview Press, 42–75.

Pavlowsky, Agnes (1998) *Hamas or the Mirror of Palestinian Frustration* (*Hamas ou le Miroir des Frustrations Palestiniennes),* Paris and Montreal: L'Harmattan.

Phillips, Anne (1993) *Democracy and Difference,* Cambridge: Polity Press.

Roy, Olivier (1999) *The Failure of Political Islam*, 2nd edn, Carol Volk (trans.), London: I.B. Tauris Publishers.

Salame, Ghassan (ed.) (2001) *Democracy without Democrats? The Renewal of Politics in the Muslim World*, London: I. B. Tauris.

Schiff, Ze'ev and Ya'ari, Ehud (1989) *Intifada: The Inside Story of the Palestinian Uprising that Changed the Middle East Equation*, New York: Simon & Schuster.

Sida (1999) *Towards Gender Equality in the Palestinian Territories: A Profile on Gender Relations*, Stockholm: SIDA.

Tamimi, Azzam (2002) 'Can Islam be secularized', www.ii-pt.com/articles.

Taraki, Lisa (1989) 'Mass organizations in the West Bank'. In N. Aruri (ed.) *Occupation: Israel Over Palestine*, Massachusetts: Belmont, 454.

Taraki, Lisa (2003) 'Islam is the solution: Jordanian Islamists and the dilemma of the "modern woman"'. In Bryan Turner (ed.) *Islam: Critical Concepts in Sociology, Vol. III: Islam, Gender and the Family*, London: Routledge, 643–661.

Tornquist, Olle (1999) *Politics and Development: A Critical Introduction*, London and New Delhi: Sage Publication.

Voet, Rian (1998) *Feminism and Citizenship*, London: Sage Publications.

WAD – Women's Action Department (1997) 'Palestinian woman … what next?' 'al-marah al-falastineyya ila ayn'. Workshop and conference proceedings, Gaza, April.

Waylen, G. (1996) *Gender in Third World Politics*, Buckingham: Open University Press.

White, Jenny (2002) *Islamist Mobilisation in Turkey: A Study in Vernacular Politics*, Seattle and London: University of Washington Press.

Zubaida, Sami (1997) 'Religion, the state, and democracy: contrasting conception of society in Egypt'. In Joel Beinin and Joe Stork (eds) *Political Islam: Essays from Middle East Report*, Berkeley and Los Angeles: University of California Press, 51–63.

Zubaida, Sami (2000) 'The trajectories of political Islam: Egypt, Iran and Turkey', *Political Quarterly* 71(Issue Supplement s1): 60–78.

Zubaida, Sami (2003) *Law and Power in the Islamic World*, London and New York: Tauris.

Just between us: identity and representation among Muslim women

Amina JAMAL

ABSTRACT *Postcolonial feminist representations of Muslim women as subjects and agents have successfully cleared a space for unsettling oppressive colonial representations of Muslim women as unchanging victims of patriarchal religion and Muslim men. This space has also brought into view new problems and issues that divide Muslim women into feminist and fundamentalists, secular and religious, diasporic and native. This paper focuses on one of the most contentious issues of Muslim women's representation: secular feminists' attempts to represent women in Islamic religious movements. In this process I examine some of the normative and ethical dimensions of feminist research as they emerged in my research with women in the Jamaat-e-Islami, a movement for religious reform and renewal in Pakistan. I reflect critically on issues in feminist research across ideological differences, incongruent locations and divergent cultural and spiritual investments.*

Introduction

'Please think carefully when you write about Islam and Muslims. After all you are one of us. We might be targeted first [the woman pointed to the scarf covering her head and face to indicate that she was talking about veiled Muslim women] but you will not be spared either,' she said.

I started my research on Jamaat-e-Islami women in 2004, just a few years after September 11, 2001 when Pakistan was fully inserted into the War on Terror as an ally of the US. The Jamaat-e-Islami is one of the most significant movements for Islamic renewal and reform in South Asia. Its founder, Maulana Abul Ala Maududi, is acknowledged as a major figure in 20th-century Islamic movements and his prolific writings on Islam, gender and Western modernity are widely read by all those Muslims who are presently referred to as 'Islamist', i.e. who seek to bring about an Islamic society through political, legal and social change.[1] In Pakistan's large urban centers, the Jamaat-e-Islami has a substantial following among women mostly of the middle classes. In addition, the public visibility of women members of the Jamaat was greatly boosted during 2002–2008, when many of them were assigned to represent the party in response to state-mandated representational quotas for women in local, provincial and national bodies.[2]

During 2004–2006, I interviewed 12 of the main women leaders of the Jamaat-e-Islami's Women's Wing in (Pakistan's major urban centers) Karachi and Lahore. This number is significant since membership in this religious movement turned political party is based upon strict selection criteria rather than voluntary enlistment. The Jamaat-e-Islami is organized around a small group of members/leaders who are expected to recruit, educate and lead a larger body of followers and supporters.[3] In Pakistan, where women's political participation is generally significantly lower than that of men, the measure of my interviewees for women's participation in organized religious politics may be considered to have implications beyond their numbers.

On this day in 2005 I had gone to the city offices of the Jamaat-e-Islami Women's Commission in Karachi hoping to meet with some core women members of the Jamaat-e-Islami who I could persuade to participate in my research. In reminding me of the perils of representing Islam and Muslim women, this woman parliamentarian of the Jamaat-e-Islami encapsulated some of the key issues and concerns that feminist researchers have debated and discussed in their attempt to make social and ethnographic research reflexive, accountable and political. Her cautionary advice to think carefully what I write about a group of women identifying as 'religious' in a world increasingly dichotomized as Islamic and secular may be read as a reminder of the context of our interactions. Her claiming of me, the researcher, as 'one of us' may be interpreted as a call to be reflective of my own identity as a Muslim woman. Her qualifying this relationship by pointing to the differences between us was a reminder to be attentive to the heavily implicated systems of power and knowledge in which our communication was embedded.

The post-9/11 local, national and global context intensified my concern for what feminist researchers consider *reflexivity* in social research, i.e. the normative and ethical dimensions of research. It also presented new challenges to my desire to embrace some guiding feminist principles for research across ideological differences, incongruent locations and the divergent cultural and spiritual investments.

It is by now well accepted that reflexivity in feminist research is not simply a matter of confessing one's location in structures of class, sexual identity, ethnicity or religion as a mode of making visible one's privilege in relation to those we are 'researching'. Indeed, informed by Foucauldian theories of power, many disparately located feminists who are grouped together under the label of postmodern or poststructuralist, relate reflexivity to a variety of strategies of making visible and taking responsibility for the power relations that sustain all projects of social research. Feminist academics and researchers, critical of conventional social science research methods, methodologies and analytical categories, have emphasized that our understanding of social and cultural realities is always already shaped by the relationship between the researcher and the researched and the location of both within larger sets of economic, political and cultural relations (Strong-Boag 1998; Khan 2001; Harding and Norberg 2005). Reflexive practices help feminist researchers keep normative questions and ethical issues at the center of their knowledge projects and guide us towards modes of understanding social reality in ways that dismantle rather than uphold fixed identities and locations as the nodal points of power.[4] Elaborating these ideas in the context of globally dispersed processes of capitalist production, political secularism and cultural modernity, postcolonial feminists scholars call for transnational practices, deconstructive strategies and intuitive cartographies in research projects involving women across geopolitical and national contexts (Grewal and Kaplan 1994). Scholars such as Gayatri Spivak, Inderpal Grewal, Caren Kaplan, Chandra Mohanty and Jacqui Alexander enable us to move beyond the politics of location and identity by proposing that we eschew traditional notions of domination and resistance in the interest of offering more complex accounts of gendered subject formation. They complicate this project even more by asking feminist researchers to understand, as do Grewal and Kaplan, that 'complex subjectivities, positions, and power relations are endemic to all groups, whether in the north, south, First World or Third' (Grewal 1988: 523). Thus, a project such as mine, purporting to study a group of 'Muslim women' is enjoined upon not only to look into questions of foundations, agency and subjectivity in their hegemonic or counter-hegemonic modes but to theorize cultural localities in Canada and Pakistan, as trans-local sites for the convergence of hegemonic cultural nationalisms and emergent patriarchies both in their secular and religious manifestations.

In this paper I revisit some of the interlinked issues and dilemmas of feminist research – politics, context, positionality, reflexivity – as I embraced them during my research on Jamaat-e-Islami women in Pakistan. While these dilemmas badger all feminist researchers, they seem to intensify when the interviewer is seen to straddle the dividing line of insider/ outsider, citizen/diasporic, First World/Third World (Khan 2007; Sultana 2007). In particular, Muslim feminists writing about their 'own' societies and cultures have expressed deep anxieties about the politics of reception of their work in a context of increased Islamophobia and widespread despair with Islam and Muslims in many western societies (Abu-Lughod 2001; Khan 2001, 2007; Mahmood 2005; Razack 2007).

Contextualizing Muslim women in a post-9/11 world

It is now almost a decade since the United States initiated a 'War on Terror' against what North American and many European leaders perceive to be a formless, stateless, borderless enemy motivated solely by an extremist (Islamic) desire to destroy western values and modes of life.[5] Pakistan, tenuously situated on the colonial cartographers' imagined borderline between the Middle East and South Asia, is considered to be both a frontline ally of western societies and a haven for all those beings – young Muslim men but also some women – who are conjured up by the term 'terrorist' in the contemporary western imagination. The gendered implications of the ongoing wars in Afghanistan and Iraq have come to be as complex and heterogeneous as the material and social effects of the conflict, since colonial representations of the Muslim women have been intensified and also overwritten by notions of gender, race, class, and religion shaped by ideas about security and civilization. It is becoming evident that conventional images of veiled Muslim women as passive or oppressed are being subsumed under an emerging image of the willfully veiled Muslim woman, who is seen to defiantly negate western liberal notions about social development and secular modernity.[6] More important, she is the figure that threatens to dis-gender the hegemonic construction of 'good Muslim' versus 'bad Muslim', which is one of the key cultural logics of the US-led global financial, political and cultural support for 'liberal' or 'moderate' Islam. Such logic brackets political and military problems and upholds theories of cultural conflict or Clash of Civilizations in which Muslims who are seen to adopt western values are consider to be 'good' while those who are overtly religious and Islamic are deemed to be anti-West and therefore 'bad'.[7] Recent scholarship has drawn attention to the harmful effects of such dichotomous constructions of East/West, religious/secular, modern/traditional and offered deconstructive critiques of the underlying systems of power/knowledge that uphold these constructed oppositions (Asad 2003; Brown 2005; Mahmood 2005; Razack 2007).

The constructed opposition of Islam versus West has further convoluted the thorny relationship between Jamaat-e-Islami women and those who may be described as secular feminists in Pakistan since politico-religious groups have their own culturalist understanding of the relationship between Islam and 'the West'. Just as political conservatives in western societies suspect Muslims of antipathy towards western values, politically conservative Muslims understand the conflicts in Iraq, Afghanistan and occupied Palestine as manifestations of a larger and longer western antipathy towards Islam and Islamic values. On many occasions I found myself enjoined upon to try to dislodge the Islam-versus-West framework of my interlocutors in an attempt to reorient them towards antiracist, progressive politics, especially feminist ones, in both Muslim majority and western societies.[8] This desire to clear the misgivings about feminism became more urgent on those occasions when my interlocutors addressed me directly as an envoy of the feminist movement in Pakistan and the West, which they often (deliberately, it seemed to me) fused together, such as in the following exchange:

Jamaat-e-Islami Interlocutor: Innocents can be put in jails in the US, innocents are killed daily in Iraq or in Pakistan but no one bothers. Yet one bomb explodes in London and within hours we are told that the perpetrators are Muslims and Pakistanis. And then in response there are [western military] attacks on masjids and madressahs [in Afghanistan]. Why do you [western feminists] choose one set of standards for yourself and another for us? When women ask you to ask us about our stance on women's issues, well take a message from us to them – ask the feminist and women's rights activists how come they are not protesting the deaths of Muslim innocents?

Amina: I must inform you that you are under a misperception – not all western feminists are supporters of the anti-Muslim sentiment or Islamophobia. They too deplore the undermining of rights of Muslims by the West; they too question the motives of those who oppress Muslims in the name of anti-Terrorism. Western feminists, even more than Pakistani women, joined the massive protests against the war on Iraq.

In almost all such exchanges, I came away feeling that I had made very little difference to my interlocutors' entrenched distrust of feminists and feminism – the West or the westernized. This distrust had been strengthened by the material effects of the global political context on the lives of Muslim women in Pakistan. Many of my interlocutors frequently recounted the local and national effects of the policy of the Pakistani government of then president Pervez Musharraf, who had committed the nation to supporting the US-led forces against the Taliban in Afghanistan. The Jamaat-e-Islami, while not classified as an extremist or terrorist group, is a strong opponent of the US-led invasions of Afghanistan and Iraq. It was evident that Jamaat-e-Islami women, who were always suspicious of the feminist movement in Pakistan, have now become even more skeptical about the agendas of Pakistani feminists that draw upon fundamental rights of citizens, universal notions of women's rights and international human rights convenants in the struggle for improving women's access to education, political participation and employment. In interviews, women recalled several new policies of the government that were introduced between 2002 and 2005 by President Musharraf, including changes in the education curriculum for government-run schools, lifting restrictions on information media and on foreign cable networks, and measures to increase women's political participation. Many of these actions were part of the government's attempts to control the influence of religious groups through what President Musharraf had termed his program of Enlightened Moderation. My interlocutors felt these were meant to curry international, mainly western favor and were ways to enhance western cultural domination of Islamic societies. This attempt to link the government's support for the War on Terror and the feminist agenda for women's rights was summed up by a Jamaat-e-Islami woman activist who said: 'The system that our government is trying to bring about merely to please Europe, America, Japan and other industrialized nations is a dangerous one'. Elaborating on this, another Jamaat-e-Islami woman remarked:

> What is happening is that there is one representation of Islam by the UN, US, feminism and so on and there is another representation in the Quran – and we tend to see as the enlightened version only that which is legitimated by the UN and US. Now even the questions of religion are going to be decided by the US – who is the US to decide what is enlightened Islam and which is not?

These repeated reminders by my interlocutors of the national–global context of our interactions were also reminders to me of the key role of political struggles and conditions in shaping my research. Throughout my study I was conscious that my Canadian citizenship, my affiliation with First World academia and the source of funding for my project served to both enable and impede my relationship with my co-religionists in the Jamaat-e-Islami. At an early meeting, one of my interlocutors, whose consent was important to the party's participation in my project, asked me what I thought about the fact that a western government funder was willing to spend so much money on acquiring information about Muslim women in Pakistan. Jamaat-e-Islami women leaders openly expressed skepticism about the interest of First World feminists, even 'insiders' in representing them accurately; but they also added that they were interested in talking to me with the hope of clearing my misapprehensions about them and their project. Indeed my interlocutors frequently imparted information to me with the stated intention that they wanted it to be communicated to a wider public to which they felt they had limited access. Our very disparate relationships to the hegemonic global systems of representation were never subtle, hidden or subsumed within the interpersonal connections or the professional relationship that we established in and through the study.

Taking note of my 'modern' appearance (in Pakistan denoted by fashionably cut *shalwar kamiz*, no head covering or face covering, professionally cut and styled hair, makeup and so on) and my Canadian credentials and citizenship, Jamaat-e-Islami women correctly identified me as a supporter of the mainstream feminist and human rights movements in Pakistan, which organize their projects around universal human rights and fundamental rights of citizens. They also associated me with the 'westernized elite classes', a term that may be used to describe a heterogeneous and economically disparate group of citizens who, for want of a better categorization, may be said to share a commitment to the discourses and traditions of western political liberalism and are somewhat familiar with western cultural expressions such as literature, arts, music, film, popular culture and so on. While all Jamaat-e-Islami women leaders that I met rejected western ideas about 'women's freedom', they were by no means homogeneous in their relationship to western modernity or the products of capitalist globalization. During the course of this research I attended many Jamaat-e-Islami meetings, public events, seminars, workshops, training sessions, and bazaars and personally interacted with over 50 women followers, supporters, affiliates, and members of the Jamaat-e-Islami in Karachi and Lahore. These women ranged in age from their 20s to those over 60; they differed in terms of economic wealth and prosperity; some wore make-up; a couple even had their hair uncovered in public; but the majority were fully veiled, including a *niqab* that revealed only their eyes when they were in any space that might include men. Differences in ethnic background, economic wealth, lifestyle, dress, personal grooming, social/political status and education levels were evident even within my selected group of 12 respondents, some of whom derived their importance because of their family connections while others had risen in the party or won respect as individuals. Regardless of their social status, political influence or economic level there was not a single woman among the Jamaat-e-Islami women that I met in this study who was more comfortable conversing in English than in Urdu. More than anything else, it may be argued, this dis-ability is an almost irrefutable means of situating a citizen of Pakistan in specific configurations of cultural and social privilege since Urdu and English are deeply implicated in ideological claims and power struggles between groups and classes in Pakistani society (Rahman 1996, 2005, 2010). Rahman's studies confirm that fluency in English is associated with a privileged educational background, modern lifestyles, and western liberal values, while Urdu is associated with values considered Islamic and resonant with state nationalism. Indeed, Rahman notes an increasing awareness among Islamic revivalists, including the Jamaat-e-Islami and under-privileged Pakistani groups, of the need to appropriate English, as it is understood to be associated with worldly success and power in the modern world (Rahman 2005). Thus, while my interviewees varied in their educational background, it is pertinent to note that they shared a common cultural social terrain that located them outside of the English-speaking privileged elite world, whether they had attended English medium or Urdu medium schools, private institutions or publicly funded institutions, whether their *shalwar kamizes* were tailored from fine imported or local fabric or inexpensive Pakistani cotton.

In reminding me of what they considered to be my duty to Islam and my Muslim identity given my access to western resources, my interlocutors also gestured toward my intermediary position between 'fundamentalism' and 'feminism'. Although they did not expect me to support their political-religious ideology and positions, I was frequently reminded that I should not add to the plethora of negative representations of the Islamist project; in turn I promised them that I would try to be as faithful as possible in representing their religious and political positions and in translating and transcribing their statements. These discussions added a sense of accountability to my work, beyond the requirement of institutional ethics and review processes, which was reflected in writing strategies in many ways. For example, since all my interlocutors were speaking as public figures expounding a political public agenda, they readily consented to being identified in my published work. Despite their consent I decided to exercise discretion in attributing statements that I considered to be potentially harmful or embarrassing for an individual speaker. This strategy was meant partly to 'safeguard' their reputation and partly out of a hope that it might temper positions and remarks that might appear alarming or militant to western readers.

However, at the same time as I try to respect and understand the religious – and, at times, anti-imperialist – underpinnings of the Jamaat-e-Islami women's project, I do so as a Muslim woman who does not identify with what is referred to as 'Islamist politics', a position within which the religion-politics of Jamaat-e-Islami women may be situated. In the South Asian context the use of Islamist, in contrast with Islamic, may be a useful way to signal a direct contrast to the traditional and devotional forms of Islam in this region.

Negotiations of faith

Our shared and disparate background complicates my study of Jamaat-e-Islami women in important ways. Like them, I was shaped by religious, cultural, educational, and political discourses that we inherited, embraced, reproduced or rejected as gendered, middle-class Pakistani citizen-subjects. Unlike my interlocutors I write from a position that I understand as feminist; like them I also lay claim to another cultural political site that is mis-referenced by the term religion. I was raised in a religious Muslim family that had an established reputation in South Asian history for being immersed in the knowledges, beliefs and practices of what is often termed 'classical', as opposed to 'modernist', Islam. While my formal education, in Pakistan and Canada, was largely in the western humanist and social science tradition, I have also received life-long training, with some degree of formal learning, in Islamic history, scriptural texts and their doctrinal implications. This training is both similar to and very different from the training and education of the Jamaat-e-Islami women with whom I interacted. Thus, in a sense that is crucial to the understanding of Islam and Muslim history in South Asia, Jamaat-e-Islami women and I represented two different, indeed oppositional, currents that became evident in Muslim politics in India in the 20th century.[9]

Islamist modernism that emerged in 20th-century British India, while a response to colonialism and Hindu nationalism, was also a fundamental challenge to centuries-old beliefs and practices of Islam in South Asia as well as its traditional knowledge producers, the *Ulema* (Jalal 2002; Zaman 2002; Alam 2004). For most of the *ulema* – even more so those allied to the mystic traditions of Islam as were my ancestors, the Jamaat-e-Islami's founder, Maulana Maududi, and his reformist project were seen as anathema to the pious and spiritual principles developed by classical Islamic scholars and embraced by ordinary Muslims since the 13th century (Robinson 2000).

I frequently identified myself to my interlocutors by referring to my family background and in the process emphasized the strong influence of South Asian mystical and devotional Islam on my Muslim subjectivity. This signaled to my interlocutors the wide distance that separated me from the Islamic position of Maulana Maududi and the Jamaat-e-Islami, and therefore their own. It situated the cultural and political differences between us not only in the comfortable contrast of modernity and tradition but also in the more discomfited realm of the religious in which Muslim identification invokes contested histories and conflicted meanings for contemporary South Asians.

These differences, which seemed to be negotiated and on occasion bracketed during the research phase of my study, seemed to intensify during the writing process, most of which was done in my parents' home in Karachi where I spend the summer. It was not that I was enabled to become 'more religious' or pious among my relatives. Rather, my living environment impeded my ability to approach my interlocutors' religiosity with the untested eyes of a researcher whose eyes are suddenly opened to the possibilities of religious subjectivity and agency. Later on, in presentations of my work to mostly western feminist academic audiences, I was often advised to be more ethnographic in my writing and provide more descriptive accounts of their religious activities and practices. Islam as a site of empowerment and as a mode of organizing one's life and everyday activities was not as new to me as it might be to researchers who are non-Muslim or not similarly exposed.[10] Muslim women's lives and experiences behind the *purdah* (seclusion practiced by Muslim women in South Asia), the practices involved in gender and sexual segregation, the rules regarding *purdah*, the nature of prayers and the minutiae of 'Islamic life' were so commonplace or familiar to me that I did not even think of them as worthy of noting or mentioning in my research log until I read about them as noteworthy points of reference in other studies (Deeb 2006; Ahmad 2009). For instance, I did not think it worthy of comment that my interlocutors always used the phrase *Sallallah-e-aleh-wasalum* (Peace be upon him) each time they uttered the name of the Prophet Muhammad. Or that my interviewees always made plans to meet with reference not simply to the clock and calendar but to the specific prayer time such as after *Zohr* (afternoon) or before *Maghreb* (sunset). The idea of operating in a time-space outside of what Anderson (1991) has called the homogeneous time of secular capitalist modernity did not confront me as an externality, since my parents' house was structured in similar manner so that lunch was always after *Zohr*, tea after *Asr* (early evening) and dinner after *Ishaa* (evening) prayers.

Whenever I mentioned some of the religious aspects of my background/upbringing to my interlocutors we became linked in an unconfirmed complicity in a commonly shared project, i.e. Islam. However, our different attachments to Islam imposed a reserve between us that made my interactions feel different from the familiarity often experienced by feminist anthropologists in their encounters with non-feminist women (Mahmood 2005; Deeb 2006). I could not think of my interaction with Jamaat-e-Islami women as anything more than a respectful debate across a deep ideological and political divide. I insisted on a certain legitimacy as a gendered Muslim subject, derived from my inherited positioning in the Urdu-speaking religio-scape of North India. It was a negotiated process as to whether, and to what extent, they were able to grant me that legitimacy.

Reflexivity compromised?

What is conventionally seen to constitute the analytical phase of a research project and the completion of field work was overtaken by regional events and political developments in Pakistan. From the middle of the last decade almost all of Pakistan, including Karachi, began to unravel through daily violence too dispersed between religion and secularism to allow any enumeration of origins. These developments strengthened my commitment to avoid replicating a dichotomy of 'pious Muslim women' and 'sinful women') in my analysis.[11] I began to unscramble some of the threads that knotted up my commitment to fundamental rights and human rights of religious or secular subjects in all contexts and my refusal to support the hegemonic impulse that was clearly evident in the Islamist project.

Working from the feminist commitment to reflexivity as a responsibility to expose, and possibly, disrupt the power differentials of researcher and research, I drew upon the critical insights provided by other scholarship on women in contemporary movements of Islamic revival and reform (Ahmed 1992; Gole 1996; Mahmood 2005; Deeb 2006; Torab 2007). Using poststructuralist, postcolonial and postmodern theories, these studies of the interrelationship of Islam, gender and modernity have enabled complex understandings of veiling, bodily practices and religious practices of women in Muslim societies and communities. From a variety of positions these scholars have persuasively argued that such practices cannot be unproblematically understood to be oppressive simply because they do not fit western liberal notions of freedom or autonomy. Approaching Jamaat-e-Islami women through the critical genealogies of the secular, the colonial and the modern was enlightening but it also felt inadequate in the local and national context of Pakistan where everyday lives are becoming unraveled by the potential violence of modernity in its religious and secular guise. It was necessary to clear a space wherein to discuss the complex interaction between feminism and fundamentalism that might ensue when gendered Islamism as agentive action becomes entangled, as it necessarily must, with the historical politics of the modernizing nation state. This was affirmed by more recent studies of self-defined Islamic women by feminists situated in Third World or Muslim majority contexts. Such studies tend to approach issues of agency and subject-formation with an eye on the overt or covert significance of Muslim women's definition of gendered piety in upholding exclusionary agendas of politico-religious groups for women and religious minorities in many Muslim societies. Sadaf Ahmad (2009) examines a women's revivalist movement Al Huda, in major Pakistan cities of Karachi and Lahore, and Shehabuddin studies the relationship of Jamaat-e-Islami to poor rural women in Bangladesh. Their work goes beyond reinstating the agency of Islamic women or disrupting the hegemonic hold of western secular modernity (Shehabuddin 2008). By drawing attention to the emergence of new modes of defining 'Islamic' and religious, pedagogical innovations and refashioning of religious ideology, these studies make it necessary to engage the relationship of contemporary Islamist movements to the classical traditions of Islam in South Asia.

Conclusion

As vexing as the question of imperialism is, there are other questions that enhance and impede accountability to the subjects of our research studies when self-identified Muslim feminists write about Islam and its assorted devotees. In the case of South Asia, these questions relate, above all, to the ongoing undermining of the discourses of classical Islam by the discourses of Islamic modernism and the resulting material, emotional, spiritual, cultural and political effects on the lives of its diverse individuals and communities.[12] Therefore, while building on the space created by postcolonial scholars, my research was persistently dogged by another question that might evade postcolonial scholars in other contexts: when some groups of Muslim women construct themselves as rightly guided religious subjects in a political-cultural space overwhelmingly identified as Muslim and Islamic, in relation to whom or what is this notion of gendered Islamic selfhood defined and sustained? Furthermore, how are we to situate their politico-religious selfhood within authoritative local accounts that consider Islamic or Muslim identity in South Asia, not as an ontological absolute, but as a historically dynamic and flexible identity with important social, cultural, and material effects on the lives of Muslim women? (Said Khan 1994; Jalal 2002; Alam 2004).

These dilemmas are not limited to South Asian Muslim women; some conceptual and political implications of these questions for feminists writing about gender and Islam in Middle Eastern contexts have been addressed by, among others, Abu-Lughod (2001). In an essay on the effects of Edward Said's *Orientalism* on Middle East feminist studies, Abu-Lughod discusses the various dilemmas facing Muslim women between challenging colonial representations of themselves and their societies, and questioning local and national institutions and structures that maintain gender hierarchies. Her important insight is that Said's work was not simply about challenging Orientalist representations of the West's Others but about the significance of these representations to ongoing projects of domination. She says this is evinced in Said's work in a persistent tension between a humanism that looks beyond cultural difference and the Foucauldian project of tracking the relationship between power and knowledge in the colonial undertaking.

Being attentive to this important impulse in Said's postcolonial analysis, according to Abu-Lughod, raises the 'uncomfortable question' (Abu-Lughod 2001: 105) that merely challenging Orientalist representations of Muslim women does not solve the key issue that concerned Said – that production of knowledge in and for the West is a means of continuing western dominance. As long as we are writing for and in the West about 'the other' we are implicated in projects that continue western authority and cultural difference. Abu-Lughod discusses various strategies by women to challenge both western stereotyping of Middle Eastern/other societies as backward/uncivilized/barbaric and also mount internal critiques of gendered power in Middle Eastern societies. She advises us to be aware that we tread 'complex grounds' and confront 'multiple forms' of injustice, none of which we can evade but must continuously challenge. She asks feminists to draw on Said's humanist and also critical stance as a 'model for the kinds of political engagements that they [feminists] inevitably face' (Abu-Lughod 2001: 112).

I support Abu-Lughod's proposal that the answer to the transnational, multiply-situated dilemmas of Muslim feminists representing Islamist women is to unequivocally reject the Islamic tradition/western modernity divide. But, like Abu-Lughod, I must ask: 'how sophisticated do you have to be to manage this?' (Abu-Lughod 2001: 110).

Acknowledgement

The research for this was enabled by a Postdoctoral Fellowship from the Social Sciences and Humanities Research Council of Canada (SSHRC).

Notes

1. I use the term Islamist, as does the extant literature on political Islam, as an ideology that resonates with other political ideologies such as socialist, communist, fascist and so on (Nasr 1994, 1996; Grare 2001; Esposito 2003). This term captures the ideological nature of movements, such as the Jamaat-e-Islami, which seek to redefine completely the nature of Islam, from a religion into an all embracing system in which the Shariah is yoked to the acquisition of political power (Nasr 1994, 1996).
2. The Jamaat-e-Islami was compelled to abandon a longstanding reservation about women's participation in public life, especially electoral politics, in order to challenge the candidates from other parties. The government of Pakistan reserved special seats for women in the elections of 2002 in compliance with CEDAW (Convention on the Elimination of All Forms of Discrimination Against Women). This was the first time that Pakistan's politico-religious parties claimed a significant performance in national elections. However, this was overturned when they suffered a crushing defeat at all levels of representation in 2008.
3. For details and a discussion of the party's structure see Nasr (1994).
4. See for example Harding and Norberg (2005); Spivak (1993, 2004).
5. Other views are evident among leaders in South American states, many citizens of North American and European societies and many Muslims around the world, who understand this war to be connected in

complex ways to the Israeli–Arab conflict and the effects of US policies towards the ongoing Palestinian struggle against Israeli occupation.

6. See for example Zine (2006). Also, Jabbra (2006); Jiwani (2005); also see the discussion of European and Turkish leaders' statement about Muslim women and religious extremism in Clark (2007).
7. For a fuller discussion see Mamdani (2004) and Zine (2006); see also Jabbra (2006) and Jiwani (2005).
8. I refer to my interviewees as 'interlocutors' as other postcolonial feminists have done (e.g. Deeb 2006) to refer to the subjects of their ethnographic projects. I consider this term appropriate for my relationship with Jamaat-e-Islami women in Karachi and Lahore since it establishes the dialogic nature of all writing and also the inevitably political character of social research.
9. For an excellent discussion of the relationship between classical and modernist Islam see Smith (1957).
10. Some of these feminist awakenings are described in Ahmad (2009); Mahmood (2005); Deeb (2006).
11. The concept of 'sinful women' is invoked here from the feminist Urdu poem 'We Sinful Women' by Kishwar Naheed (1990), and is intended to acknowledge those Muslims, such as mystical poets, artists, musicians and others who have for centuries challenged the strict moral code of puritanical Islam. See Ahmad (1991).
12. For a good discussion see Jalal (2002); Zaman (2002); Robinson (2000); Minault (1982); Mumtaz (1994), Metcalf (2005); Needham and Rajan (2007).

References

Abu-Lughod, Lila (2001) 'Orientalism and Middle East feminist studies', *Feminist Studies* 27(1): 101–113.

Ahmad, Rukhsana (1991) *We Sinful Women: Contemporary Urdu Feminist Poetry,* Lahore: Women's Press.

Ahmad, Sadaf (2009) *Transforming Faith: The Story of Al-Huda and Islamic Revivalism Among Urban Pakistani Women,* Syracuse: Syracuse University Press.

Ahmed, Leila (1992) *Women and Gender in Islam: Historical Roots of a Modern Debate,* New Haven and London: Yale University Press.

Alam, Muzaffer (2004) *The Languages of Political Islam: India 1200–1800,* Chicago: The University of Chicago Press.

Anderson, Bendict (1991) *Imagined Communities: Reflections on the Origin and Spread of Nationalism,* London: Verso.

Asad, Talal (2003) *Formations of the Secular: Christianity, Islam, Modernity,* Stanford, CA: Stanford University Press.

Brown, Wendy (2005) 'Subjects of tolerance: why we are civilized and they are the barbarians'. Paper presented at Seminar on Gender and the Global Locations of Liberalism, Institute for Social and Economic Research and Policy, Columbia University, Spring, www.iserp.columbia.edu/downloads/brown.pdf, accessed 19 February 2005.

Clark, Sevda (2007) 'Female subjects of International Human Rights Law: the Hijab debate and the exotic other female', *Global Change, Peace and Security* 19(1): 35–48.

Deeb, Lara (2006) *An Enchanted Modern: Gender and Public Piety in Shi'i Lebanon,* Princeton and Oxford: Princeton University Press.

Esposito, John L. (2003) 'Introduction: modernizing Islam and ee-Islamization'. In J.L. Esposito and F. Burgat (eds) *Global Perspective. Modernizing Islam: Religion in the Public Sphere in Europe and the Middle East,* London: Hurst and Company, 1–14.

Gole, Nilufer (1996) *The Forbidden Modern: Civilization and Veiling,* Ann Arbor: University of Michigan Press.

Grare, Frederic (2001) *Political Islam in the Indian Subcontinent: The Jamaat-e-Islami,* New Delhi: Manohar Publishers and Distributors.

Grewal, Inderpal (1988) 'On the new global feminism and the family of nations: Dilemmas of transnational feminist practice'. In Ella Shohat (ed.) *Talking Visions,* New York: MIT Press, 501–530.

Grewal, Inderpal and Kaplan, Caren (1994) 'Introduction: transnational feminist practices and questions of postmodernity'. In *Scattered Hegemonies: Postmodernity and Transnational Feminist Practices,* Minneapolis and London: University of Minnesota Press, 1–33.

Harding, Sandra and Norberg, Kathryn (2005) 'New feminist approaches to social science methodologies: an introduction', *Signs: Journal of Women in Culture and Society* 30(4): 2009–2015.

Jabbra, Nancy W. (2006) 'Women, words and war: explaining 9/11 and justifying U.S. military action in Afghanistan and Iraq', *Journal of International Women's Studies* 8(1): 216–235.

Jalal, Ayesha (2002) 'The religious and secular in pre-colonial South Asia', *Daily Times Pakistan,* 21 April, www.dailytimes.com.pk, accessed 10 July 2006.

Jiwani, Yasmin (2005) 'The Great White North encounters Sept 11: race, gender and nation in Canada's national daily, the globe and mail', *Social Justice* 32(4): 50–69.

Khan, Shahnaz (2001) 'Between here and there: feminist solidarity and Afghan women', *Genders* 33, http://www.genders.org/g33/g33_khan.html, accessed 20 July 2008.

Khan, Shahnaz (2007) *Zina, Transnational Feminism, and the Moral Regulation of Pakistani Women*, Vancouver: UBC Press.

Mahmood, Saba (2005) *Politics of Piety: The Islamic Revival and the Feminist Subject*, Princeton, NJ: Princeton University Press.

Mamdani, Mahmood (2004) 'Good Muslim, bad Muslim – an African perspective', http://www.ssrc.org/sept11/essays/mamdani_text_only.htm, accessed July 2004.

Metcalf, Barbra D. (2005) 'The study of Muslims in South Asia'. Presented at the University of California at Santa Barbara, 2 December, http://www.columbia.edu/itc/mealac/pritchett/00islamlinks/ikram/part0_metcalfintro.html, accessed 28 February 2008.

Minault, Gail (1982) *The Khilafat Movement: Religious Symbolism and Political Mobilization in India*, New York: Columbia University Press.

Mumtaz, Khawar (1994) 'Identity politics and women: "fundamentalism" and women in Pakistan'. In V.M. Moghadam (ed.) *Identity Politics and Women: Cultural Reassertions and Feminisms in International Perspective*, Boulder, San Francisco and Oxford: Westview Press, Inc., 228–242.

Naheed, Kishwar (1990) 'We sinful women'. In *Beyond Belief: Contemporary Urdu Feminist Poetry*, Rukhsana Ahmad (trans.), Lahore: Women's Press, 22–23.

Nasr, Syed Vali Reza (1994) *The Vanguard of the Islamic Revolution: The Jama'at-i Islami of Pakistan*, Berkeley: University of California Press.

Nasr, Syed Vali Reza (1996) *Mawdudi and the Making of Islamic Revivalism*, New York: Oxford University Press.

Needham, Anuradha Dingwaney and Rajan, Rajeshwari Sunder (eds) (2007) *The Crisis of Secularism in India*, Durham and London: Duke University Press.

Rahman, Tariq (1996) *Language and Politics in Pakistan*, Karachi: Oxford University Press.

Rahman, Tariq (2005) 'Passports to privilege: the English-medium schools in Pakistan', *Peace and Democracy in South Asia* 1(1): 24–44.

Rahman, Tariq (2010) 'Language problems and politics in Pakistan'. In Paul Brass (ed.) *Handbook of South Asian politics*, Oxford: Routledge, 232–246.

Razack, Sherene (2007) 'The "Sharia Law Debate" in Ontario: the modernity/premodernity distinction in legal efforts to protect women from culture', *Feminist Legal Studies* 15(1): 3–32.

Robinson, Francis (2000) *Islam and Muslim History*, New Delhi: Oxford University Press.

Said Khan, Nighat (1994) 'Reflections on the question of Islam and modernity'. In N. Said Khan, R. Saigol and A. S. Zia (eds) *Locating the Self: Perspectives on Women and Multiple Identities*, Lahore: ASR Publications, 77–95.

Shehabuddin, Elora (2008) *Reshaping the Holy: Democracy, Development and Muslim Women in Bangladesh*, New York: Columbia University Press.

Smith, Wilfed Cantwell (1957) *Islam in Modern History*, New York: The New American Library.

Spivak, Gayatri C. (1993) 'Scattered speculations in the question of cultural studies'. In *Outside in the Teaching Machine*, New York and London: Routledge, 255–284.

Spivak, Gayatri C. (2004) 'Terror: a speech after 9–11', *boundary 2* 2(Summer): 81–111.

Strong-Boag, Veronica (ed.) (1998) *Painting the Maple: Essays on Race, Gender and the Construction of Canada*, Vancouver, BC: UBC Press.

Sultana, Farhana (2007) 'Reflexivity, positionality and participatory ethics: negotiating fieldwork dilemmas in international research', *ACME: An International E-Journal for Critical Geographies* 6(3): 374–385.

Torab, Azam (2007) *Performing Islam: Gender and Ritual in Iran*, Leiden and Boston: Brill Academic Publishers.

Zaman, Muhammad Qasim (2002) *The Ulama in Contemporary Islam: Custodians of Change*, Princeton and Oxford: Princeton University Press.

Zine, Jasmin (2006) 'Unveiled sentiments: gendered Islamophobia and experiences of veiling among Muslim girls in a Canadian Islamic school', *Equity and Excellence in Education* 39: 229–252.

'Bahar Nikalna': Muslim women negotiate post-conflict life

Diia RAJAN, Deepa DHANRAJ and K. LALITA

ABSTRACT *This paper is based on a three-year research project entitled* Minority Women Negotiating Citizenship.[1] *Conceived of in the aftermath of Gujarat 2002, the project studied 75 life-history narratives of Muslim women survivors of communal violence in Gujarat, Hyderabad and Mumbai, in order to map their everyday experiences of negotiating survival, marginalisation and exclusion. While analysing our material we found that our preliminary organising or analytic categories – victim, agent, Muslim, woman, class, location – could not contain the negotiations and fluid 'subjects' of the narratives. The most useful analytic concepts and tools were those being used by the women themselves in their narratives, such as* bahar nikalna *and* sambhalna. *These women negotiate a hostile state, poverty, violence, communalised politics and public spaces, and increasingly belligerent community structures on an everyday basis. The complexity of 'identity' and 'agency' as they emerge in the narratives, and the syncretic nature of their everyday negotiations, challenge the rigidity of existing frameworks and dominant discourses on issues of Muslim identity and citizenship.*

Introduction

The 2002 pogrom in Gujarat saw untold and innumerable acts of violence perpetrated mostly on Gujarat's Muslims. Thousands were killed, mutilated, and raped, and thousands more displaced from their homes – and remain displaced even today. The Gujarat government neither prevented the violence nor prosecuted the perpetrators. Today, the government does not even acknowledge the horrors of 2002.

When we visited Gujarat in 2003, we witnessed several depositions of women who had survived violence to take on 'agentive roles' in negotiating various institutions seeking justice, compensation, livelihood, and survival for their families and their community. Women were engaging with and being engaged by not only family and the state (in terms of claiming justice), but also NGOs/CBOs, religious organisations, markets, and 'communities'. These engagements were taking place in a site particular to the post-conflict/post-violence situation – a destabilised, volatile and incoherent quotidian space.

It has been the overwhelming experience of poor women from such marginalised communities that they are consistently unrecognised, unheard and unacknowledged by state institutions. However, it is not only negotiations with the state, but equally those with family and community, that need to be resourced in order to map women's lived experience in post-conflict situations. Women as victims, women as agents of peace, and women's roles in defending/rebuilding communities have been studied and written about in conflict literature. What is often missed out in the study and analysis of conflict and its impact, are the complex everyday experiences of poor women seeking accountability, justice, and very often, mere survival.

This project studies life-history narratives of Muslim women's everyday experiences of accessing and engaging family, community, markets and state in order to map and understand the agentival processes of negotiating survival, marginalisation and exclusion in post-conflict situations. The state's involvement in the violence, non-responsiveness if not open hostility towards affected Muslim communities, and the increasing marginalisation of these communities paralleled by the consolidation of a dominant Hindu ideology, foregrounds the issue of citizenship for India's Muslim communities.

Citizenship, then, provides us with a relevant frame of reference within which to examine and map these women's experiences and articulations. We believe that in order to unpack women's agency and their lived experience of citizenship it is important to examine their life-experiences in their *own* articulations. This helps us gain a sharper picture of women's negotiations across spheres of family, community, markets and state and how these negotiations create, impede and impinge on women's voice and agency.

What happened in Gujarat was unprecedented in many senses, but is not a unique moment in India's history. While our initial intention was to look at the everyday experiences of Muslim women in Gujarat post-2002, we expanded the geographic scope of our research to include the cities of Mumbai[2] and Hyderabad, which have had long histories of communal conflict. As part of the study we have conducted 75 narrative life-history interviews. With a few exceptions of women from middle-class political/professional backgrounds, most of our interviewees are poorer Muslim women. The primary focus of the study has been urban spaces, except in the case of the Sabarkanta and Panchmahaals districts of Gujarat, which experienced the same intensity and forms of violence, displacement, and other-community hostility, as the urban areas.

Analytic frameworks

Citizenship has emerged over the past two decades as a cross-disciplinary discourse, engaging and informed by political, feminist, critical, and development theories as well as development practice. Classically, the concept of citizenship has been variously theorized as status, practice, and identity, premised on the relationship between the individual and the nation-state, where the nation-state is the constant spatial frame of reference. Contemporary discursive engagements with citizenship have pushed the boundaries of formalist frameworks towards conceptualising citizenship as both status and practice, as an expression of voice, and a relation of accountability (Yuval-Davis 1997; Mukhopadhyay and Meer 2004). The question of identity, and consequently of group rights/recognition, and inclusion/exclusion has been central to theoretical engagements with citizenship, with many contemporary theorists arguing that access to and experience of citizenship is framed by the specific location(s) of particular subjectivities (Mamdani 1996).

The emergence of questions of identity, exclusion, and contemporary theoretical attempts at opening citizenship to nodes of difference, have critiqued the centrality of the universalising concepts of nation and state to the construction of citizenship. Recent political and feminist theories are repositioning citizenship as a concept that includes negotiating patriarchal power-relations in spheres 'other' to the state (Menon 2004). Development discourse, informed by feminist theory, positions citizenship as a useful organizing concept to look at women's role in the public domain and their experience vis-à-vis structures of power.

For the purposes of our study we drew on the feminist and development conceptualisations of citizenship as voice/agency and relations of accountability, and attempt to source these in both public and intimate familial spheres. As a disclaimer, we would like to state upfront that we have not studied or engaged with the juridical notion of citizenship and what it entails; with the 'status' of the Muslim population as a whole and its position vis-à-vis the Indian state; or with the formal concept of justice and justice mechanisms. We are also aware that the subjects of this study do not belong to a monolithic Muslim community (or *qaum*) but are a heterogeneous group belonging to different sects, castes, classes and linguistic groups.

It is also important to note that we have not dealt with issues of Muslim personal law, Islam as religion or politics, or the question of the 'Muslim identity' at great length in our study. While we did not set out to overlook these issues we found that most narratives did not engage with these questions in depth. Questions of changing Islamic practices, principles and politics, personal law and political issues of identity were discussed, if at all, on the margins of the narratives.[3]

In the narratives we do not find, or seek to find, women speaking to the formal concept of citizenship (for example only a couple of women actually used the term citizenship/*nagarikta/shehriyat*).[4] In our analysis of the material we use concepts arising from the narratives, such as dignity/*izzat*, belonging/*watan*, identity/*haisiat*, and justice/*insaafi*. In the narratives, these concepts often signify values and experiences of 'citizenship'. Dignity (or the lack of) – of the individual, family, community; belonging – not only to the 'nation' but to the larger heterogeneous community, to the 'soil'; identity – of their own self-worth, recognition and respect by others; and justice – as a juridical and ethical norm, as acknowledgement of *in*justice, are all central to the experiences of everyday struggle in our narratives. These articulations not only demonstrate how constitutional citizenship is experienced, but more importantly point to how women's various negotiations seem to constitute a normative citizenship.

In our research, negotiation implies not only a conscious process of accessing and engaging with individuals and institutions but also the everyday management and handling of mundane situations. This has implications for our understanding of agency, not only as leading to structural or larger political transformations, but also as pushing for transformations at intimate, individual and localised levels.

> ...agentival capacity can also be entailed in acts that are neither about change nor about continuity, but about introducing minute internal displacements and mutations into the discursive regime in which they are articulated. Such acts may appear to be inconsequential to most participants and remain invisible to most observers. They do not have to contradict the political and ethical parameters of the system and, importantly, may even allow one to preserve the possibilities, promises, positive ideals, and ethical values of the system while avoiding the negative and oppressive constraints within which these are articulated. (Yurchak 2006: 28)

In engaging with Muslim women's everyday experiences of power and violence, our research foregrounds the concept of agency. While most scholarship has tended to conceptualise agency in the binaries of authority/resistance, dominance/subordination, in the formulation and analysis of our research material we have drawn on re-conceptualisations by anthropologists such as Talal Asad, Saba Mahmood, and Laura Ahearn, who explore agency 'within semantic and institutional networks that define and make possible particular ways of relating to people, things, and oneself' (Asad 2003: 78).

We find Saba Mahmood's work on women in the Piety Movement in Egypt insightful in its sourcing agency 'not only in those acts that result in (progressive) change but also those that aim toward continuity, stasis, and stability' (Mahmood 2001). In order to attend to the concept of agency in contexts informed by religious/cultural traditions Mahmood argues that 'if the ability to effect change in the world and in oneself is historically and culturally specific (both in terms of what constitutes "change" and the means by which it is effected), then the meaning and sense of agency cannot be fixed in advance, but must emerge through an analysis of the particular concepts that enable specific modes of being, responsibility, and effectivity' (Mahmood 2005: 14).

We are aware that Mahmood's configuration of agency, in the context of her work, is framed by a space, defined by a set of norms, and articulated by a piety particular to the Egyptian women's Islamic revival movement. Indeed, our effort is to push beyond Mahmood's argument, which continues to situate agency within an individual 'subject', consciousness, will or 'desire'. Laura Ahearn's definition of agency as the '...socio culturally mediated capacity to act' (Ahearn 2001: 112)[5] acknowledges the various dynamics – both macro and minute – which impact the creation and interpretation of agency. While keeping in mind her warning that this is a 'provisional' definition that needs further elaboration, we find her work useful in that it enables us to look at the complex interplay of individuals, institutions, politics and discourse, in reading agency.

In the preliminary presentations and discussions on our research material, we fielded several questions on the appropriateness of our using the concept of agency. The primary discomfort with this concept seemed to be that it signifies a self-aware positive act seeking social or political transformation. The women we spoke to were certainly agentive in this sense, consciously seeking and fighting for positive change in many aspects of their lives. However, we feel strongly that the smaller unselfconscious acts of engaging with everyday life also constitute agency. Mapping out agency in this textured way enables us to critically grapple with the complex question of what constitutes the 'Muslim woman in India' today, especially in a context where 'the Muslim woman', across dominant political discourses, is read as a uni-dimensional identity.

'I began to see the world for what it is...'

Many of our interviewees, across the locations, have lived through at least two violent conflicts. However, the particular event that marks their lives in an indelible way is the one that causes a rupture in their everyday lives. This rupture manifests itself as complete displacement – physical, economic, domestic and emotional. In every narrative there is a particular event that is memorialised as the one that caused a rupture of this magnitude, completely changing their lives. *'Voh fasaad ke baad dimaag khul gaya'* ('after the violence I began to see the world for what it is'), said one woman in Mumbai; we heard similar statements in many interviews and conversations.

Most narratives mention stress created by subterraneous violence created by low-intensity humiliation even prior to the event. To quote one of our interviewees: '*Babri Masjid*[6] and 2002 didn't happen in a vacuum, there was a context for that ... which was this everyday humiliation which many people (Muslims) have experienced in many different ways ... the feeling of hurt for Muslims is very strong'. We find recollections of these experiences in memories of childhoods spent with non-Muslim friends, in schools, colleges, public spaces, government offices, hospitals, banks, in the buying, consuming and sharing of food, finding and renting houses in non-Muslim localities, and in references to appearance and standard of living. These experiences were seen as stray instances of discrimination at the hands of a few 'bad people'. However, in the process of renegotiating post-event life many women begin to read these prior experiences as a central part of the process that provided the context for the event.

Women themselves explain this experience of rupture with statements such as 'riots happened earlier but we went back to our homes with dignity' (*riots bhi hote the magar izzat se ghar jaate the*), indicating the difference between earlier incidents of violence and the one event that caused complete displacement. Rupture, as we understand it from women's articulations, is not only caused by complete displacement, but also by, as it were, a rupturing of consciousness. *'Voh fasad ke baad dimaag khul gaya'* refers to this process. Women, who in their own words were confined to 'private' socio-political spaces, begin to engage with issues and questions they had previously not considered.

The immediate experiences of targeted violence are often the catalysts for the forming of a particular critical consciousness. The blurring of the distinction between mobs and police, the knowledge that the police were abetting violence; women overheard police telling rioting mobs that they had 48 hours to do whatever they wanted, and they faced verbal abuse from police. The realisation that the violence was not a confined localised incident but a well-coordinated attack on *all* Muslims – *'musalman identify kar ke mare... masjid mein aa ke mare... topi dekh ke mare'* ('they identified a Muslim and killed... went inside the mosque and killed... saw the skull-cap and killed') – and the witnessing of sexualised, emasculatory, relentless 'hyper' violence perpetrated on men, women and children.

The experience of targeted violence, the knowledge of state complicity/apathy, and the resulting trauma and displacement, forge the beginnings of a critical education where women begin to confront issues and concerns – of justice and survival – with which they had previously not engaged.

In the narratives, we find women using interesting articulations to refer to their experiences in post-violence contexts. These organic articulations have the intersectional potential to deal with complexities of the experiences being described, which other formal categories do not. The concept of *bahar nikalna* ('going out') is one of the articulations we attempted to unpack in order to look at women's own understanding of their negotiations and capabilities, and the politics of their situations.

In a post-violence situation, women find themselves economically and socially 'orphaned' by the death or disabling of male family members. Consequently they have to abandon traditional practices of immurement to work outside the house and negotiate public spaces and institutions. In doing so, they become *be-asra* (literally 'without shelter/support') and *bahar nikli hui aurat* (a woman who has left the confines of four walls). The majority of the women interviewed in this study identify themselves as *bahar nikli hui.*

Having to confront or negotiate with police and other government authorities is another compelling need that necessitates women's stepping out. In the immediate aftermath of violence, women are often the ones to seek medical aid for the injured, compensation from authorities, and negotiate law and order machinery to safeguard their properties and families. In many instances, families send their women out to deal with these issues because they are afraid that men will be subjected to further violence. In fact, across locations we find that men and children are deliberately kept confined to the house.

> I never used to go out like this or talk to anyone outside the house ... ever since our bad times started I have learnt to talk to everyone. There is no one else to handle our problems ... I have to deal with it all, the police and jails and everything...

It is not necessarily the case that the women who perceive themselves as having left the house *bahar nikli hui* in post-violence situations never actually stepped outside their homes prior to the rupture. Many of them had worked outside their homes, and accessed marketplaces and public institutions. However, the difference is that in post-violence situations women come out of their homes to shoulder responsibilities on behalf of their men and their families without any male protection or company.

For many women, being *be-asra* or a *bahar nikli hui aurat* is not necessarily a negative way of looking at themselves, but is used as a metaphor, a necessity of their lives, and perhaps even as the social norm/category they must now inhabit. Many women also have a sense of pride in what they have achieved as *bahar nikli hui aurat. Bahar nikalna* is also used to signify a shift or change in the consciousness of women. Many speak about a changing sense of self that came about as a result of going out of the house and dealing with varied public institutions and spaces. They point to an increasing confidence, an awareness and understanding of the changing dynamics of their immediate surroundings.

For *bahar nikli hui* women, especially those who are also *be-asra*, there is an added stress on continuing to inhabit the norm of being a 'good Muslim woman'. The vulnerability and insecurity of their lives, and the increased dependence on support from community structures and *jamaats*, results in an heightened anxiety of being alienated if they do not conform in some measure to the ideal of the 'good Muslim woman'.

The women we interviewed often locate themselves in, and speak from, a religious/cultural space; however, the experiences being narrated engage with several socio-economic, political and institutional contexts. These women negotiate a hostile state, poverty, violence, Hindu-ised politics and public spaces, and increasingly belligerent community structures on an everyday basis. This experience, coupled with a profound sense of a loss of dignity, belonging and family, is experienced in individualised contexts as violence.

In negotiating these contexts, women are required to constantly engage with both the dominant political as well as the Islamic constructs of Muslim (womanhood). The inhabiting of 'public' spaces and the inhabiting of social and cultural norms are concomitant processes. In our study, we find women's actions and articulations in all spheres impinge, alter, and challenge established representations of Muslim women across 'secular', communal and Islamic discourses. The 'minute displacements' of everyday negotiations discussed in the following section lay out the complexity of being and belonging.

Negotiating being and belonging

In the post-violence context, where as *bahar nikli hui* women they are dealing with numerous public and familial spaces and situations on an everyday basis, they speak of *sambhalna* (negotiating/managing), which takes on three distinct meanings: it refers to the negotiation of situations, people, and relationships at multiple levels across both public and familial spheres. It can also refer to the mundane everyday managing, supporting, dealing with and taking care of family and immediate environment. Lastly, it is often used in the individual sense of the word (as opposed to the external negotiations indicated above) as possessing a critical understanding of one's own location especially vis-à-vis social and political relations.

Used in these senses, *sambhalna* also extends in many cases to developing a knowledge of household economy, the value of work, commodities, raw materials and markets, professional skills; bureaucratic, legal and judicial (mal)functioning and red-tape; real politics at the community and state levels.

Noor, a young woman widowed during the violence of 2002, feels a sense of being *be-asra* very strongly and realises she has no choice but to be a *bahar nikli hui* woman:

> If we don't go out now what will we earn… what will we eat… we have to go out, make friends with children, with the old, with the young, with men… with every human being. If we don't make friends with people we cannot progress… neither will I be able to educate my children nor feed them, neither look after my home and family nor deal with society…

Noor has identified 'friendship' as a strategy for survival, as a possible replacement for lost community and family relationships of support. Building and sustaining these relationships is a key aspect of *bahar nikalna*. When Noor's maternal grandfather died a few years ago, she took on the responsibility of organising the entire funeral. She invited the *jamaat*,[7] all her relatives and neighbours, and borrowed 20,000 rupees at high interest to meet the funeral expenses at a time when she had no job and no help from anyone. Even though no one in the *jamaat* or her family offered to help her she organised this funeral both out of obligation, as the one who must now look after the family, as well as to keep her relationship with the *jamaat* and her family intact:

> so I brought the money and looked after the *jamaat*… the children and the family … I don't have anyone's support neither father nor brother … not even a husband … if I have someone it's the *jamaat*.

As *be-asra* and *bahar nikli hui*, Noor faced and continues to face a lot of sexual harassment and taunting from people in her own community as well as those in the market. All women who participate in public spaces – especially those who earn money from working outside their homes – face hostility, ranging from taunts to active harassment. All of them have encountered being called loose women, having abusive language used against them and their children, and being approached by men (from their community as well as outside) as sexually available. Noor is extremely pained that even women in her community question how she earns money, accusing her of prostitution, instead of appreciating how hard she works to feed her children. She is aware that many women have turned to sex work and is sympathetic to their circumstances.

> The market is filled with spit (*market jhoota thuk se bhari hai*) … the world brings women to this … when a good-looking woman goes to work men don't leave her alone.

Unlike Noor, Almas Begum is not *be-asra*. Her husband, who has been unemployed since the violence, is supportive of her work and makes sure to accompany her to her workplace and back everyday. But she still sees herself as a *bahar nikli hui aurat*:

> Nobody in our family [women] works only I do … my husband cooperates and lets me work … men in his family are different … they say you [women] should not stand at the door, you should be secluded, if the vegetable vendor comes you should only stick your hand out … forget about the hand my entire being is out!

Almas Begum explained to us that even though (or maybe especially because) she is a *bahar nikli hui aurat* she conducts herself with modesty: 'My modesty is in my eyes [she views the world with modesty] … I will never do something that will make someone point a finger at me…' Almas's firm notion of being modest (*sharam rakhna*), however, did not prevent her from becoming a karate black-belt. With unconcealed pride she narrates two incidents when she used her karate skills; once to shield herself against a molester on a public bus and once to teach a lesson to an abusive male teacher in her daughter's school.

In a context defined by the conditions and politics of displacement and violence, the nature and organisation of the 'community' undergoes significant change. Experiences of brutal targeted violence and an antagonistic state attitude towards Muslims are pointed out as reasons for the increasing insecurity within Muslim communities. Living within the confined boundaries of single-community ghettos and colonies, not having easy access to community spaces or institutions on the other side of the 'border' defining their localities, and a vigilant police presence which keeps an eye on everyone's movements and activities, heightens the sense of insecurity in Muslim neighbourhoods. This is most evident in all urban neighbourhoods, with varying degrees of intensity. This insecurity makes Muslim communities belligerent towards the state, other communities, and often towards their own members. When the belligerent attitude is turned inwards, it mostly focuses on women – taking the form of sexual policing and the enforcing of cultural norms.

One of the manifestations of this growing insecurity is the increased presence and mobilisation of conservative schools of Islamic thought. These *jamaats*, like the *Tablighis*, focus on 'pure' Islam influenced by the practices of Islam in Saudi Arabia. These schools of thought regard South Asian Islamic cultural practices – such as visiting *dargahs*, offering *fateha*, and placing *chadars*[8] and flowers on the bodies of the dead – as un-Islamic. Other cultural aspects that are considered anti-Islamic are music, singing, dancing and films. For some women, for whom many of these cultural practices are part of their religious identity and way of life, these new impositions are often unacceptable. However, many of them seem to find a way around the opposition of their husbands, sons and mullahs, to continue practising Islam the way they want to.

Many women, especially in the cities, talk about their sons joining *jamaats* and becoming overtly religious and trying to bring the entire household into the *jamaati* fold. While women understand that *jamaati* activities provide young men – who have no access to 'secular' spaces – with a space to meet and make meaning of their lives, they also feel burdened by the demands of their sons to conform to the ideal of being a 'good Muslim woman', i.e. wearing a *burqah* and keeping *purdah*. Women in rural Gujarat do not as yet seem to face similar pressures from their families and communities. However, the pressures of keeping 'family honour' and modesty continue to limit and modify what women are able to achieve in public spaces. This was most openly talked about by poorer women in Mumbai, and some areas of Vadodara and Hyderabad.

Memories of life prior to the rupture become more important in this context. Several women recollected with nostalgia and longing the rich and varied neighbourhoods they lived in before being forced into homogeneous, insecure colonies and ghettos. They regret the loss of community bonds – not just amongst Muslims but equally with their Hindu neighbours – the sense of 'belonging to the soil', belonging to the *vatan*,[9] and the richness of living in heterogeneous communities. Not a single narrative refers to the concept of a Muslim *qaum* or universal community; the narratives always refer to community in terms of their immediate geographic locations and kinship ties.

Accountability, acknowledgement, justice

When women do 'come out' to take leadership roles, representing the voice of women to the community, and representing the community to the state/'outside world', they do receive support in both subtle and overt ways. Speaking of how her relationship with male representatives of the communities she worked with changed over time, Suraiyya – a feminist social activist – says:

> They suddenly changed their opinion of me … they realized that I do have some space in my heart for the community. Perhaps their impression of me was as an elite feminist who had no care for the community … but things changed. Men and *Maulanas* have sat and talked with me … they have invited me to many meetings. All this definitely changed only after 2002. I never saw anything like this happen before … before that they had never invited me like this, saying 'come, sit'. Probably, before 2002, they had no need to talk to people like me or human rights organizations.

There seems to be a concerted effort on the part of Muslim communities, and the more moderate of community religious representatives, to seek out civil society organisations. Similarly, Muslim activists – who like Suraiyya had operated within a very 'secular' ideal prior to events of violence – have begun actively to engage with religious leaders and representatives in their community-level work. This kind of engagement between male representatives of traditional organisations and women activists has impacted in a positive way their understanding and accommodation of each others issues, needs and challenges.

Women like Suraiyya have also experienced the subtle communalisation of civil society, in their changed attitudes towards Muslim friends and colleagues in the aftermath of communal violence.

> From the start I was not ritualistic, I have full faith in Islam but I wasn't able to do *namaaz* five times a day, even then they [civil society colleagues] felt that I am a Muslim, so there was a change in their attitude … It was very strange some people wanted to call me for meetings because I was a Muslim woman and some people did not want to call me for meetings because I was a Muslim woman!

> I thought I had become a feminist but finally had to accept that I was a Muslim...

> I am a Muslim but I am being reminded that because I am a Muslim I have to move house, I am a Muslim so I have to move my office, I am a Muslim so I will lose my non-Muslim staff, so after 2002 I took a conscious decision that I should work with Muslim women.

Sultana and Arifa are middle-aged women who started their 'public life' in the aftermath of the Godhra violence. They were both active organising committee members of the Godhra relief camp. Although Sultana and Arifa are critical of the State's partisan and hostile treatment of Muslims – by law and order, administrative and medical mechanisms – they have taken every opportunity to engage with all institutions to get justice. The scale of the suffering, listening to the daily narratives of what people had been through and the realisation that there was going to be minimal state response, led to a very rapid political education of what it was to be a Muslim citizen. Initially, Sultana and Arifa were mainly occupied with addressing immediate survival needs; now they have stepped into a wider realm of demanding accountability and justice from the state.

Sultana and her husband, an important religious leader in Godhra, have also been working with POTA[10] cases for the past few years, taking on the Herculean task of mobilising resources from within the community to provide financial support to the dependents of the 70 accused persons from Godhra, and to fight their cases. Sultana keeps abreast of the dates of hearings and adjournments, and with Arifa organises discussions on court proceedings and legal strategies with the entire community. They have sworn that not one vote will be cast from Godhra until the POTA accused are released. These are conscious, self-aware arguments – Sultana does not let the narratives of suffering stand alone as self-explanatory; she always frames them by her understanding of the role of institutions.

These women are not only fluent in matters of the law, but also have a profound understanding of how state mechanisms and politics function and what skills they need to negotiate these institutions. There are several such examples of women coming out to fight their own and others' battles to hold the state accountable for relief, compensation and justice. Sultana and Arifa illustrate, yet again, the syncretic nature of these negotiations which simultaneously draw on ethics, norms, and resources across religious, secular and juridical registers.

Many women, with or without familial support, came forward to depose in front of state-appointed commissions of enquiry, like the Nanavati Commission[11] in Gujarat and the Sri Krishna Commission in Mumbai, and at public fora organised by civil society organisations everywhere. These depositions were made with tremendous personal courage, often at the risk of their personal well-being, because they felt morally bound to make their voices heard.

> I have given my testimony in Nanavati Commission as well ... That day when I went there to speak in the court, the *Chhaare* [the *Chaara*[12] men who had attacked her neighbourhood] had also come there and they started asking me 'Nadira, why have you come?' That day all the people I knew and who knew me were there in the court, so I didn't give my testimony ... So, I went again on another day and I gave my testimony...

The failure of the state, first to protect the communities and then to provide justice, gives rise to two kinds of responses from women. On the one hand they seek retributive and compensatory justice when and where they can. On the other they also seek a moral justice, from the state, civil society and the media, in the form of acknowledgment and apology.

Acknowledgment is especially important to women in Gujarat, who have been told time and time again by the state government that the carnages of 2002 never took place. The denial of the complicit state government, in the face of the thoroughly documented evidence provided by several national and international fact-finding missions and NGOs, creates a context where there can be no hope for justice – either formal or as acknowledgment/apology.

Hamidaben, in Vadodara, accosted Mr Lyngdoh – the then Chief Election Commissioner – when he was on a tour of violence-hit areas in Vadodara before the elections of 2004. She stopped him on the street and said 'you have to come with me ... don't listen to these lies'. She challenged the official police version that the area had not been affected by violence, and demanded that Mr Lyngdoh 'see the truth': to see the houses where people had not returned, to see the Muslim policeman's house which had been burnt, to see the extent of the real devastation.

When a certain Mumbai paper carried a story on Behrampada[13] being a hot-bed of underworld activity, with bomb factories being run by Muslim foot soldiers of the Dawood Ibrahim group,[14] Begum, a resident of Behrampada, leading a group of women from the neighbourhood, decided to act. Frustrated and angry with the demonisation of their neighbourhood as a haven for terrorists and criminals, they invited the journalist who wrote the story to visit the area, and took him on a detailed tour to show him the ordinariness of Behrampada. He was asked to retract his story and offer them a public apology, which he did.

Seeking justice, in these narratives, is not restricted to direct action vis-à-vis institutions of law, or to notions of compensatory or retributive justice. Similarly, accountability is also not configured only in the framework of citizenship, as a legal mechanism, but addresses all the social and political relations implicated in the context. Women's negotiations in claiming justice and accountability therefore, simultaneously engage with state mechanisms, civil society initiatives, community and family relations.

Conclusion

Early in the study we found that our preliminary organising or analytic categories – victim, agent, Muslim woman, class, location (even in terms of sectarian affiliations) – could not address or indeed contain the experiences, negotiations, and fluid 'subjects' of the narratives. Muslim women negotiate a hostile state, poverty, violence, communalised politics and public spaces, and increasingly belligerent community structures on an everyday basis. In order to understand the complexity of issues such as 'identity' and agency in these narratives we have to re-think our existing analytical tools and frameworks. Over the course of working with and analysing this material we found the most useful concepts and tools were those being used by the women themselves. We have discussed a few of these organic analytic tools in this paper.

The experience of targeted violence, the knowledge of state complicity/apathy, and the resulting trauma and displacement, forge the beginnings of a critical consciousness where women begin to engage with issues and concerns – of justice and survival – with which they had previously not engaged. In most instances the catalyst for this critical consciousness is the ascribed dominant construct of 'Muslim', which women come up against every day. This dominant political construct of both 'secular' and communal politics is confined to socio-cultural and religious dimensions, configuring the 'Muslim woman' as a unidimensional figure operating solely within a religious paradigm.

This construct of Muslim identity extends to the dominant framing of Muslim citizenship. Thus, we find debates on Muslim issues in India have focused largely on questions of personal law and rising fundamentalism; the supposedly oppressive and retrograde practices of Islam which prevent its members from joining 'modernity'; and the alleged anti-national pan-Islamic aspects of the community. These debates leave no space to accommodate the articulations of the women in our study. The syncretic nature of their everyday negotiations, which draw simultaneously on secular, religious and juridical norms and resources, challenge the rigidity of existing frameworks and dominant discourses on issues of Muslim identity and citizenship.

Notes

1. This project was conducted between 2006 and 2009, and it was supported by the International Development Research Centre (IDRC), Ottawa, Canada.
2. The most violent riots in Mumbai took place between December 1992 and January 1993, in the immediate aftermath of the destruction of the *Babri Masjid* on 6 December 1992. These were by far the worst riots in Mumbai's history, claiming close to 1000 lives and creating a permanent vicious rift between the Hindu and Muslim communities of the city. Hyderabad has seen intense communal conflict in 1948, briefly in the 1980s, and most virulently throughout the 1990s.
3. Using a semi-structured interview method we consciously avoided asking leading questions. Women who spoke on these issues brought them up in an organic way, usually in relation to their everyday experiences, especially vis-à-vis family and community relationships.
4. The italicised Hindi/Urdu terms used are drawn from the narratives; the English equivalents either precede or follow the Hindi/Urdu throughout the paper.
5. We would like to thank our reviewers for their valuable comments and for drawing our attention to the important work done by Laura Ahearn.
6. On 6 December 1992, the *Babri Masjid*, a mosque of historical significance, was demolished by a mob of Hindu nationalists from all over the country. The demolition of this mosque, the preceding rhetoric and the following nationwide violence, is regarded as the turning point in the communalisation of Indian politics.
7. Any congregation can be referred to as a *jamaat*; in South Asia *jamaat*s are usually caste-based or sectarian associations, religious/political associations or congregations.
8. A *dargah* is a tomb of a Muslim saint; *fateha* is the practice of making an offering of food to the prophets/saints; a *chadar* is the offering of a ceremonial cloth to the dead.
9. *Vatan* can mean nation, village, 'birth-place', or an emotional concept of belonging.
10. The Prevention of Terrorism Act (POTA), an anti-terrorism legislation enacted by the Indian Parliament on 28 March 2002. This law was used extensively, especially in Gujarat, to illegally detain a huge number of Muslim men. Owing to the gross misuse of this law by various state governments, it was repealed in 2004. However, those arrested under POTA continue to be detained.
11. The Nanavati Commission was set up by the Gujarat government in May 2002 as a commission of enquiry into the 2002 events of violence.
12. A Gujarati tribal community instigated by local political forces to participate in the largescale violence against Muslims in 2002; members of this community were mobilised to carry out the attack in Naroda-Patiya.
13. One of the Muslim-majority neighbourhoods in Mumbai.
14. Dawood Ibrahim is considered to be the don of the Mumbai underworld and the mastermind behind the 1993 bomb blasts in Mumbai, thought to be in retaliation to the violence of 1992–93.

References

Ahearn, Laura (2001) 'Language and agency', *Annual Review of Anthropology* 30: 109–137.

Asad, Talal (2003) *Formations of the Secular: Christianity, Islam, Modernity*, Stanford: Stanford University Press.

Mahmood, Saba (2001) 'Feminist theory, embodiment, and the docile agent: some reflections on the Egyptian Islamic revival', *Cultural Anthropology* 6(2): 202–236.

Mahmood, Saba (2005) *Politics of Piety: The Islamic Revival and the Feminist Subject*, Princeton: Princeton University Press.

Mamdani, Mahmood (1996) *Citizen and Subject: Contemporary Africa and the Legacy of Late Colonialism*, Princeton: Princeton University Press.

Menon, Nivedita (2004) *Recovering Subversion: Feminist Politics Beyond the Law*, Delhi: Permanent Black.

Mukhopadhyay, Maitrayee and Meer, Shamim (2004) *Creating Voice and Carving Space: Redefining Governance from a Gender Perspective*, Amsterdam: Royal Tropical Institute.

Yurchak, Alexei (2006) *Everything Was Forever, Until It Was No More*, Princeton: Princeton University Press.

Yuval-Davis, Neera (1997) 'Women citizenship and difference', *Feminist Review* 57: 4–27.

Piety, music and gender transformation: reconfiguring women as culture bearing markers of modernity and nationalism in Bangladesh

Samia HUQ

ABSTRACT *The rise in an intense, textually-based piety, which has become increasingly prevalent in many circles in Bangladesh in the past decade, sees music as taking away from an ideal pious disposition, and therefore considers its removal from everyday life as a requisite to becoming a good Muslim. The removal of music is critically looked upon by secular Bengali Muslims, where singing, especially songs of the Nobel Laureate Tagore, is equated with cultural pride and Bangladeshi nationalism in the secular-liberal, especially the intellectual imaginary. The shunning of such music is thus tantamount to shunning 'Bengaliness' and a source of anxiety for the nationalist. In this article, through a deeper exploration of women's struggles of and sense of achievement in giving up music, I argue that for the women in pursuit of piety, what the act of giving up music speaks to is inner changes that enable them to critically reflect upon roles and relationships that have long been the defining features of a particular kind of middle class, Bengali, feminine self. The paper argues that shunning music is taken as a medium through which women critically rethink their positions at home, reconfigure old roles and expectations and come out of the process with a greater sense of control and ability to write their own identities as Muslim wives and women.*

Introduction

Arifa: People's hearts [*mon*] are soft. Songs give rise to a lot of feelings, even if the lyrics are not necessarily lewd [*oshlil*]. It takes the mind to an imaginary place that is removed/disconnected from reality. If there isn't sufficient awareness [*shochetonota*] and fear [*bhoy*] of Allah in one's heart, one may be tempted to act on one's imagination, and there in a sin will be committed.

Kakon: Music [*gan*] should not arouse sexual desires in a person. Being in some imaginary world with lots of sexual feelings aroused can be dangerous.

Reema: That's why, what is allowed is girlfriends getting together and singing at weddings or other festivities.

Munira: I like listening to Nazrul's songs. Some days, I play some Nazrul songs to relax and unwind. Islam doesn't have a problem with songs per se, but with instruments.

Kakon: How can you have songs without instruments? What are you saying?

Munira: (looks guilty) That's also true… [*tao thik*].

The above conversation took place between educated and financially solvent women who meet in a religious discussion circle in Dhaka, Bangladesh. The main intent of these women congregating is to actively seek and cultivate piety, a piety the women project as modern, pro-women and detached from the religiosity associated with Islamist groups. In enacting and cultivating a modern, politically neutral piety, women conceptualize music as an unnecessary evil due to its ability to arouse sexual, romantic emotions. Even if the lyrics are 'safe', it fosters the creation of a creative space that competes with the focus required for the cultivation of piety. However, the fact that many Bangladeshi women who are cultivating piety and bear outer marks as testimony to it would reject music is met with very sharp reactions. In a casual conversation, a university professor said, 'Who are these women? It sounds a little excessive to me!' Another woman said, 'Why do women have to resort to such extremes? What is this about? Haven't women been religious in the past? We've always been a God-fearing people, but we also are a people with a rich cultural history'. Thus, giving up music is obviously alien to the cultural repertoire of the Bangladeshis that provide such critiques. This article deals with the pious dictate of giving up music pitted against a discussion of the significance of music in the cultural and national landscape.

In this paper, I argue that giving up music and the negative reactions to it can be understood on two levels. The first is the political level where music represents certain ideals of secularism, progressive nationalism and therefore modernity in the public, political imaginary. However, I point out that the manner in which music and singing by women plays into constructs of nationalism and modernity does not accompany a corresponding understanding of women's sense of self, which brings me to the second level at which discarding music is to be understood – the very personal level at which women understand what it means for them to be women.

In Bangladesh, 'middle-class' families employing a tutor to teach their young children, especially their daughters, to sing, has been quite a common cultural practice. The majority of the women that are a part of my research claimed that they have, at some point in their lives, learnt to sing either from a tutor who came to the home, or that they attended one of the reputed schools for singing. When asked about the changes adopted in the pursuit of piety, interestingly, giving up singing and any other kind of association with it came up strongly as one of the activities they have been struggling to discard. In this paper, I delve into the architecture of discarding music in general and singing in particular, with women's accounts of the corollaries that accompanied its removal from everyday life. In going beneath the surface of religious injunctions, the paper explores how women conceptualize singing as having gendered them in particular ways and what is happening to the construction of the feminine self now that the practice of music is no longer a part of their social and familial landscape. In tracking the changes of the feminine self through engagement with cultural practices such as singing, the article sheds light on how norms of piety override and change older gendered norms and gives new meaning to what it means to be a woman, simultaneously problematizing dominant notions of modernity and nationalism.

Music and singing in Bangladesh

In Bangladesh, members of the urban middle class make a distinction between religious and secular music while taking up singing. If women want to sing religious songs, the genre of choice would generally be *hamd* or *nath*.[1] While singing *hamd* or *nath* is a common part of religious rituals such as *milads*,[2] or the commemoration of the prophet Muhammad's birthday, this genre of music is not cultivated as an artistic form. Rather, when we see *hamd* or *nath* being performed on television, it is done by artists who are known primarily as singers of Nazrul or Tagore's songs. Nazrul is Bangladesh's national poet, and the Nobel Laureate Rabindranath Tagore, although from West Bengal, is a part of most middle-class lives and homes through his works of literature and songs. When women cultivate music as an art form, it is usually classical Indian, Tagore and Nazrul that they choose to train themselves in. The significance of such singing – notably the branching out to Nazrul and/or Tagore – has to be understood on the basis of the complex and variegated ways in which both Nazrul and Tagore have occupied spaces in the political and national imaginary.

Born to different faiths, the works of both Kazi Nazrul Islam and Rabindranath Tagore called for tolerance between faiths and communities, especially in the spirit of freedom from colonial rule. Gulam Murshid (2007) argues that in many respects, Nazrul was more revolutionary, where he called for a religion based on humanity that would transcend all kinds of organized religion. As a result of his critical stance towards organized religion, he often incurred the wrath of Muslims in his era, earning the label of '*Kafer Kazi*' (Kazi the infidel). However, ironically, when India was being divided along religious lines, the demand for a separate nation state for Muslims saw Nazrul represent the national struggle of Muslims. However, the Nazrul that was appropriated as part of this struggle was a divided and partial Nazrul, where only particular works of his were privileged while his syncretistic devotional songs (*shyamsangeet*, *kirton*, etc) were completely overlooked. Murshid writes (in Bengali), 'The same Nazrul who in the 1920s was insulted as an emissary of Nimrod, Pharaoh and Satan, became a pro-reform Muslim in the 1950s' (Murshid 2007: 167). According to Murshid, Nazrul's Muslim identity, at the complete elision of his pro-humanity/ universal religion stance, was in fact, a means of keeping the Bengali masses distracted and away from Tagore (Murshid 2007: 166).

Rabindranath Tagore posed a threat to the unity of a people that was brought and kept together through recourse to religious solidarity. By drawing on the 'Bengali' ethos of the East Pakistanis, Tagore's work had the power to validate a collective identity of the East Pakistanis through means other than Islam. In other words, as the Muslim identity ceased to be unifying, there was apprehension amongst the Pakistani ruling elite that the Bengali Muslims may draw on their Bengaliness to assert rights that the authorities were intent upon keeping from them. The seeds of discontent and the claim for a separate cultural-linguistic identity had already been sown in the language movement of 1952, when the Pakistani army opened fire on, and killed, a troupe of protesters who took to the streets against the ruling that Pakistan will have only one state language and that would be Urdu.[3] The Bengali need to be validated through language made the authorities acutely aware of the deep resonance of the 'Bengali' amongst the Muslim Pakistanis of Bengali origin and ethnicity. The State thus began an overt campaign suppressing works and celebrations of Tagore. Some examples include the banning of Tagore's songs on national radio, the festive commemoration of Tagore's birthday, and even debates over whether universities should include Tagore's work in their literature syllabi (Murshid 2007: 138).

In the midst of such obstacles, Tagore and his work gained a new significance. Murshid writes, 'Tagore's name became the mantra of protest. The government's resistance to Tagore had exactly the opposite effect. The people of East Bengal, much more than ever in the past, made Tagore their very own. Not through reading him in text books, the Bengali Muslims owned Tagore through protest and struggle'[4] (Murshid 2007: 138). With Tagore as an emblem of ethnic identity and a burgeoning nationalism, the cultural struggle made headway in several ways. For example, there were mass movements by intellectuals and cultural activists that culminated in the formation of institutes such as *Chhayanaut*.[5] Then there were women holding up the torch of cultural assertion by wearing the sari and *teep* (mark on forehead) as well as singing Tagore's songs (Kabeer 1991). Tagore's songs were sung by both men and women. However, it was women's practice that came to symbolize subversion and resistance. In other words, in keeping with the manner in which women are subsumed within dominant narratives on modernity and nationalism, respectable women's bodies became a legitimate site of national contestation and representative of nationalist agendas (Siddiqi 2009: 17). Thus, women were brought to the fore of the political struggle that would give birth to a new nation.

The 'constructed' idea that women were agents of modern nation building overlooked several things. First, women's projection as culture bearing resisters of state supremacy unfortunately did not accompany any corresponding interest in women's rights in general

(Siddiqi 2009: 16). Next, the relationship between singing as a cultural act and women's agency in undertaking it is made to appear natural to what Bengali women do. However, scholarly work on the topic as well as personal insights prove otherwise. Sumanta Banerjee, writing about the changing place of popular culture in the lives of 19th-century Bengali women argues that once a Bengali woman became educated, gained access to western literature and climbed up the class hierarchy to become a *bhadramahila*, she distanced herself from women of the lower classes and the forms of popular culture they would engage in together. Her new class positioning and new cultivations meant that 'A *bhadramahila*'s cultural pursuits acquired a private chamber character. The collective gaiety of a *panchali* session was narrowed into individual compositions to be appreciated by the husband and his friends, or to be printed in magazines to be read by the educated few' (Banerjee 1989: 167). Thus, cultural activities may have become more 'sophisticated', but they also became more private and therefore distinct from the more public cultural pursuits of lower class women, which were now looked upon unfavorably as vulgar and licentious. The *bhadramahila*, through her cultural undertakings, espoused and manifested a particular brand of womanhood (Banerjee 1989: 165). When cultural acts then come out into the public space, as they did with Bengali women's protest to Pakistani authorities, what happens to that womanhood? Did it no longer risk being vulgarized because the times had changed? I feel that the elapse of time is probably not an adequate explanation as casual conversations with women undertaking cultural acts such as singing and dancing do reveal the tensions and debates around the appropriateness of Bengali Muslim women's performances. Many argue that women who were performing and in public were already from 'good enough' families, and thus had immunity. However, the question remains: what was the immunity against? What are some of the tensions around notions of womanhood, femininity, women's bodies, their chastity and sexuality that had to be negotiated before women were allowed to become public culture bearers of political protest? In the dominant narrative on women partaking in promoting ethnic solidarity and contributing towards the birth of a new nation, an understanding of these negotiations, i.e. women's own formulations of and negotiation in their sense of self, do not come to the fore.

Culture, state and a debated Islam

With inadequate insights into ideas of femininity and womanhood, upon the independence of Bangladesh, the dominant discourse on nationalism marched on to take an even stronger stance against the parochial form of Islam that the Pakistani state had been trying to impose to crush the movement for Bangladesh. This stance first banned all kinds of religious forces from participating in the formal political arena, leading to a ban on the Jama'at-e-Islami which had collaborated with the Pakistani junta against the liberation of Bangladesh (Ahmed 1994). Next, the constitutional adoption of 'secularism' was also taken as an official marker of the new nation's religious openness.

While many were quick to equate secularism with the absence of religion, the state reacted and defended its position by arguing that secularism did nor refer to a lack of faith, but rather promoted a more open and tolerant kind of Islam. This Islam was to be compatible with markers and bearers of cultural identity. In addition, the term referred to the 'exclusion of communal forces from politics' and the freedom of all individuals to practice their respective faiths in private (O'Connell 2001). However, critics were not appeased. The dialogue between government/liberal forces and the masses was tantamount to a debate on whether the place Islam had been given in the state represented the sentiments of its 'faithful' citizens. In the midst of these debates, especially by the end of the Mujib era, 'Muslim assertiveness in public life' was on the rise (O'Connell 2001: 189).

The assertion of the Muslim self is seen as an 'assertion' primarily because the Islamic identity gained greater public presence. One of the public manifestations was a critique of the role of music and performance in private as well as public life. An extreme example of this was the bombing of the largest and most highly attended *Pohela Boishakh* (Bengali new year) celebration in Dhaka in 2002. The JMB – a militant outfit that seeks to establish the rule of *sharia* in the country – claimed responsibility. Thus, 'giving up culture' is often equated with these extremist, Islamist positions, and thereby it is a source of great surprise when 'modern', 'educated' women who are clearly not terrorists are drawn to such injunctions. While the general tendency is to equate these prohibitions with the moralizing rhetoric and consequent activism of Islamists, I argue that there is greater insight to be gained by looking deeper – at how these injunctions speak to the shaping of the self.

In post-liberation Bangladesh (1971–present) women's role in representing modernity and nationalism has continuously and systematically elided women's own sense of self as they are made to carry forward development initiatives, receive micro credit and become entrepreneurs, contribute to export earnings through their labor in the ready-made garments (RMG) industries (Kabeer 1991; Siddiqi 2000). In the omissions of essential understandings of womanhood, there were several stakeholders. Western donors had their priorities to privilege the development agencies, while the State straddled between appeasing the donor and lending support to increasing Islamist rhetoric influenced by the oil-rich Middle East. Thus, the discourse on women 'emphasized women's needs, leaving the relationship between needs and notions of womanhood unexplored' (Jahan 1995: 103). Given this lacuna, the different stakeholders pressed for their different ideas and initiatives, underlying which there were different notions of womanhood, albeit not made explicit as part of their plan.

The Islamist position on women, again represented principally through the Jama'at-e-Islami, is based on the ideology that 'gender roles are divinely ordained, as legitimized through religious tradition and laws. In this view, men and women were created unequal by God, so any attempt to bring equality is heretical' (Jahan 1995: 104). Such a view thus renders gender hierarchy fixed, thereby precluding any possibility of transformation that benefits women. In living religious precepts, women thus become automatons, always accepting both the precepts as well as conditions of subordination. The stringency of such a discourse on women has been linked to the 'Islamic onslaught' on women by way of attacks on NGOs,[6] *fatwas*,[7] and the famous Taslima Nasrine[8] case. Thus, the Islamic discourse on women and gender is seen as a retrogressive one that is oppressive and anti-modern.

Existing ethnographic accounts of the decreased practice of singing in rural Bangladesh argue that injunctions on performance and singing also affect the self in negative ways, leading to a loss of an avenue for articulating and expressing subversion of gender relations (Gardener 1998). Built into this conclusion are normative assumptions of ideal gender relations and the nature of subversion. Resistance and subversion have long been tropes through which women's agency has been analyzed within anthropology as well as in feminist accounts (Abu Lughod 1990). However, as Saba Mahmood points out, when this formula of agency is applied on women enacting piety, we see that agency describes a 'whole range of human action including those which may be socially, ethically or politically indifferent to the goals of opposing hegemonic norms' (Mahmood 2005: 9). Thus, Mahmood proposes that rather than approaching norms through the lens of subversion, we focus on the variegated ways in which norms are inhabited, revealing the grammar of particular actions, enabling us to discern the nuances that mark the consolidating as well as subverting aspects within each action.

Through the cases I present, I delve into the grammar of giving up music by exploring women's motivations and the intended and unintended consequences of the action. In unearthing the mechanics of discarding music at a deeper level, I argue for the importance of understanding religious injunctions not (only) on the basis of uncritical equation with Islamists' moralizing (often violent) presence in the public space, but (also) through a closer engagement with how the pursuit of piety speaks to formulations and notions of the self. In these formulations that I will argue are ripe with strife, deliberation, assertion and a sense of fulfillment and triumph in overcoming obstacles, there is a reformulation of womanhood that women feel very positive about. Given such assertive and positive transformations of the self, I ask for a problematizing of the dominant view that giving up music is anti-progress, anti-modern and thereby anti-nation.

Religious injunctions

The women from the lesson circles believe that the need to stop listening to and singing songs derives from a Hadith that asks the believer to refrain from *'lawh'* – an Arabic word denoting pastime or diversion. In the Hadith, *'lawh'* specifically contains instruments of music. However, the Hadith also mentions emotions that arise out of listening to the instruments of music, and by extension music in general. Listening to music falls into the same category as devouring others' wealth, treacherous behavior, and drinking wine. Music and immoral behavior are thus intermingled.

In my research groups, based on the degree of involvement with music, I have found women belong to three camps. The first consists of the practitioners: the ones who have trained in a particular genre of music; the second is the passionate listener: the ones who spend significant amounts of time listening to music and claim to have (had) a real emotional connection to their preferred genre of music and songs; and third: the ones who are less dependent on it, but who claim to listen just because it is on, for whom it may function as 'background noise'. It was the practitioners and the avid listeners for whom music held the greatest appeal. It was this category that struggled the most in removing it from their everyday lives. Women look back to reflect on the positive effects discarding music has had on their sense of self, morality and ability to assert themselves to family members. Through the two in-depth cases I present, I will shed light on what aspects of moral behavior the abandoning of music has redressed, and the manner in which leaving music has reclaimed the morality of the female, Muslim self.

Arifa: gender relations and the inner self

Arifa married into a family that was very musical. Her 'Bengali' identity was strengthened by the fact that her father was killed by Pakistani forces in the independence war of 1971. Her father-in-law was known to her father, and therefore was sympathetic about the fact that she had lost her father in the war. Arifa says that her father-in-law – a lawyer – was a serious but fair man and was respected by his peers for his principles. Of all the members amongst her in-laws, he was the most religious. However, Arifa's mother-in-law was from West Bengal, and was the one who brought music into the home. Arifa says, 'My mother-in-law really enjoyed music and would host musical soirees (*jolsha*) in our home – but only when my father-in-law was away in the village'. Here, we see the not-so-uncomfortable coexistence of a 'strict Islamic' way with the 'Bengali' inclination towards music – a Bengali-ness that is bolstered by its association with West Bengal. While Arifa's mother-in-law waited for her husband's retreat to the village in order to 'live out' her Bengali-ness, it is noteworthy that she was allowed to do that – signaling a mutual respect, even when inclinations were different.

It is in this setting that Arifa took up music. She says that her husband was generous with money and extremely interested (*shoukheen*). He played the guitar and his record (LP) collection filled several rooms in the house. A few years after their marriage and the birth of her first child, when she wanted to pursue singing, he was obviously very encouraging. Arifa's musical genre of choice was Tagore's songs (*Rabindra Sangeet*). She first trained with a tutor at home, and within a few years employed Sadeq – one of the best Rabindra Sangeet artists in the country – to train her at home. She claims that her voice had really developed well and that Sadeq was very pleased with her progress. As her musical guru (master), Sadeq began to promote her at cultural events. Arifa says,

> I was totally caught up in singing at these events. Sometimes rehearsing for them meant that I had to stay out late, and put in long hours into practicing at home as well as outside the home. My children were small. There were times when I would not be able to nurse my baby properly because I had to attend rehearsals. Sadeq was making arrangement so that I could cut a record and become a radio and television artist.

This is the point at which her husband intervened, accusing her of overdoing it. He asked her to stop performing at cultural events and to restrict her singing to the home and familial circles. Arifa was outraged. She angrily asked her husband why then he had allowed her to train and come this far, to which her husband responded that singing was primarily for herself. She argued,

> How can I sing for myself. That doesn't make sense. Music is inherently for others. Songs are sung as gifts [*upohar*] to be presented to others. If one cultivates one's talent for singing, she must spread [*bikashito kora*] that talent [*protibha*] around. I realized that it is possible to hold another person in a spell through music. And what's wrong with that, as long as one's intentions [*uddessho*] were noble – and mine always were.

Arifa's last sentence is very telling, revealing the sexual tension that performative singing carries. However, Arifa also redeems her role as a performer by de-essentializing performance and lending it credibility by bringing in the moral character of the performer. In other words, while Arifa insists on taking her singing beyond the personal, she contains its sexual potential and connotations as it traverses from private to public through a recourse to intentions and motivations – inner states that exist as distinct from the act of singing. In other words, Arifa's retort against her husband was founded upon the argument that singing per se was not problematic; and while, through her talent, she imparted music as a gift, she could still continue to be a virtuous woman, and thereby continue to sing.

The point on which Arifa felt unable to negotiate with her husband centered not on the question of her morality, but her domestic responsibilities. The fact that she herself brings up the fact that she would sometimes not be able to nurse her baby, or stay out late (implying the neglect of duties such as being around for the family at meal times), signals the hold these duties have over women's lives. Interestingly, when her husband was trying to curtail her singing, the dialogue that transpired between the two reflected a conflation of one with the other. In other words, by singing in public Arifa was being negligent towards the home and family, and by extension risking her morality. While Arifa felt strongly about defending her moral character, she was less sure about the domestic duty part.

Arifa, albeit unsure about her performance as wife and mother, did not take her husband's dictate (that she should sing only at home and for herself) lying down. She reacted in a passive-aggressive manner by not singing at all and telling Sadeq, her teacher, that she was not home whenever he came to the house to give lessons. Arifa felt tremendous resentment towards her husband. Hers was a classic case of middle-class propriety where women's roles and sexual morality are intertwined in a way that women find difficult to separate and break out of. She felt powerless in front of her husband, and fought back by resisting and rejecting the opportunities (with limits) that he was allowing her.

Soon after the upsetting and defeating episode over her musical pursuit came Hajj. Arifa says, 'Hajj was the start of the miracle' that marked her entire journey through piety. It was at Hajj that Arifa felt overwhelmed with emotions and awe. After Hajj she started to read and think and change. She says, 'I now realize that my husband was right about the singing'.

From a woman who initially resisted her husband's dictates and even rejected his conciliatory advances, what are we to make of Arifa's present stance that her husband had been right all along? It is important to point out at the outset that Arifa's admission of her husband being correct comes from her obedience not to him, but what she believes are God's dictates. In her mind she had not conceded to her husband, but to God – a concession that would have been made even if her husband had not reacted the way he had. To strengthen this point, Arifa does not forget to add that, after Hajj, her husband, whose LP collection was too large for the many rooms that housed them, also gave up listening to music. In other words, the giving up of music applied equally to both spouses, thereby removing from it the burden of representing gender hierarchy and nullifying the notion that it was a mere re-enactment of a male (husband's) injunction to women. She asserts that the post-Hajj transformation was even more severe in her husband. However, after going through an intense period, he has reverted to some of his old ways. Arifa says, 'due to the influence of his family, many of his worldly fancies [*shoukhinota*] have found their way back into his life. He now buys CDs again and listens to music', while Arifa describes herself as going from 'strength to strength'. Thus, interestingly, while her husband is the one who wanted her to curtail her singing, they both showed strength and conviction and left music by yielding to divine authority. However, it was Arifa and not her husband who has been able to keep the conviction alive. It is she who now advises him on what is good and beneficial – not for the home, or in this world, but for his soul.

I asked her what she gained from letting go of music. In response, Arifa dispelled the original argument she had made in favor of music by asserting an a priori interiority, separable from the effects of music. She says,

> I know and always knew that music had the power to create feelings and emotions. For example, when we sang at the music school that I used to attend in the early years, I used to see the wife of a prominent actor whose life was public information. She never said anything but sang and cried. Maybe she was thinking of her marriage, or her autistic child. So, music does make you feel things – I saw that with my own eyes. It can heal as well as open the self up to wounds and vacuums, where the lyrics of the songs, rather than words of God fill in the gaps.

I asked Arifa how damaging the pursuit of music could have been; she replied,

> Maybe the time away from my husband and children would have just made me more indifferent to my duties. Once indifference crept in, who knows what could have happened – especially given the power music and singing had on me – even though I denied it at the time. Of course, music aroused emotions and sensitivities – why else was I so enamored by it? Maybe the discord would have broken my home [*shongshar*].

Here, we see Arifa's behavior in two phases of her life. The first phase is marked by the absence of the cultivation of piety and the prevalence of the desire to sing. The focus at the time ended with singing. The 'extra-musical association'[9] (De Bano 2005: 445) was overshadowed by pulling in *uddeshho* or intention, which Arifa at the time considered to be noble. Once religion enters the scene, we see that intentions are questioned in light of her new found knowledge. Thus, 'intention is not only a means to faith and a way of establishing relationship with God, but is also a rational and controlling process' (Torab 1996: 241). Her reconfigured intentions thus not only control her world but also give new meaning to old practices and responsibilities.

Arifa's assertion that the abandonment of music may have saved her home through a refocusing on domestic duties may sound like a strengthening of patriarchal understandings leaving little room for change. However, for Arifa, while many of the duties consisted of the same activities, the assumptions underlying them and the expectations shaping them changed. She thinks back to her own life and claims that she was highly praised for her singing. The praise she received was also extended to her other abilities – such as her cooking, her ability to maintain a good home, design clothes, dress nicely, etc. Arifa says, 'I behaved as though I was unfazed by the praises, and acted humbly. But inside I was gloating, which I now believe must have also fuelled my endeavors'. She now claims to be embarrassed by it all. She says,

> Now I avert praises. It is due only to Allah. Behind the satisfaction of receiving praises lie other not so pleasant things – such as competition. I began singing around the same time as my husband's sister [*nonod*] and his brother's wife [*ja*]. While I would never admit it at the time, we were all very competitive. I now think that the competitive streak was disguised but also pushed us all to excel, at the end of which we were never happy about others' achievements, and therefore never fulfilled with our own. Is that the person I am supposed to be? Before I used to just cook and cook, and constantly invite people for dinner parties. I used to say that I do it because I like it. Everyone praised me for being a good housewife [*shangsharik*]. But who has asked women to be SO into their homes [*shangsharik*]? Surely not Allah – because he knows us and knows what in our hearts motivates us. Having returned from a difficult world [*kothin jogot*], and fought with my heart [*mon*], my *nafs*, through the labor [*porisrom*] of my *nafs* (and not the labor of cooking, entertaining and singing), I am now content and fulfilled [*poritripto*]. In that world [*jogot*], the motivations came from competition, and the need to show off, within and outside of the family. The natural progression of competition was jealousy [*hingsha*].

Abandoning music has made Arifa reflect upon the other tasks she undertook, categorizing them all not as duties/acts in the private or public sphere, but as acts from a particular and peculiar world (*jogot*) that affected the inner-self in negative ways. It is the inner-self that she feels able to have affected. And having affected positive changes, she feels that the relevance those acts had as forming her role and thus herself does not carry the same weight. Thus, she still cooks and invites people to visit, and even takes pleasure in doing so, but the grammar of these acts is very different. By making a conscious effort of averting praise, she feels that her roles and duties, while serving practical needs, are primarily for Allah, whereby she is a mere instrument of Allah's will. However, her submission to Allah's will has come through labor – 'the labor of *nafs*' – and it has enabled a transcendence of power relations between herself and her husband and his family, that were once instrumental in defining the various acts she undertook in her role as wife, in-law and woman.

Suhaila: does my husband have *haya* towards his beautiful wife?

Much like the other participants of the Quran learning circles, Suhaila grew up in a home where religious rituals such as prayer and fast were performed and festivities observed. However, other aspects of her day-to-day existence were not influenced by religious doctrine or dictate. She attended a co-education school, had different kinds of friends and went to parties. Her home was extremely musical, where both parents were into singing and dancing. Both Suhaila and her sister were trained in Indian classical music since childhood. Suhaila's sister went abroad and became a popular recording artist. Suhaila, who was very beautiful, was married off to an older, wealthy businessman after her A-levels. Upon marriage she proceeded to have three children, travel the world with her husband, host dinner parties and musical soirees and perform other social and familial duties. Through these activities, all of which together in combination can place demands on one's time, Suhaila kept up her music. She practiced with a teacher every morning, and once a year, for three months she and her sister would pay to bring in a well-known maestro from another country to train with him. She says, 'Singing was my passion. It was my piece of heaven and when I sang I felt like I was carried away to another world, a better place'. Other than giving her psychological peace, singing also gave her recognition amongst her family and friends. Her talent marked her out from the rest of the crowd. Although she never sang professionally, she would often sing for a gathering of friends. Her husband was very proud of her singing. She narrates, 'He not only loved to hear me sing, he also likes to show off my talent to our friends'. Thus, like Arifa, Suhaila also acknowledges the role of praise and recognition as a catalyst to (performative) singing.

With her engagement with religion she learnt that singing was not allowed, and that all musical instruments are forbidden. She says, 'Giving up singing was a very difficult thing for me and it took a long time for me to feel comfortable with the decision not to sing. It had become a habit, and it was the one thing that I really excelled in. And yes, it felt great when people said that I have the voice of a nightingale'. Suhaila said that she was not able to give it up overnight. Initially, she claims that she used to go by the dictate that no one else (especially men) should hear her. She then would sit alone and sing for herself. However, she says, 'It simply was not working. The fact that I sang, I kept wanting to do more of it. It was an addiction. The more I sang, the more I wanted to sing, and I knew that one day the addiction would land me in front of others again. I knew that I had to have God's words – his music to fill my heart with, and decided to do recitation [*telawat*] of the Quran'.

When I asked her why her heart should be filled with only the Quran, and why she did not continue to sing the devotional songs whereby music and singing could have been a permissible part of her piety, Suhaila replied the following:

> I did not have enough of an understanding of Allah. Without that, whenever I sang, whatever the contents were, I would always fall into the traps of *shaitan* [Satan]. The singing would be personal and deep – but only and always about me. However engrossed I was in the singing, even if I was in front of no one – my pleasure would come from my deep awareness of my own abilities by which I carried a tune, which in turn transported me somewhere else. I couldn't move away from the 'I' in the singing. The condition of *Telawat* – that it shouldn't be so melodious that the melody rather than the message transfixes helped me through my *jihad*[10] of being torn between wanting to sing and giving it up, and to be able to keep myself balanced within it.

Unlike Arifa, whose initial impetus to give up music came, much to her displeasure, from her husband, for Suhaila the situation was quite the opposite. Suhaila's husband enjoyed her singing, both for himself as well as the pleasure of others. She says,

> When I decided to give up singing, I was worried about how my husband would take it. One day when I refused to sing in a gathering, he was fuming with anger. When we came home he brought the harmonium to our room, put it on the bed and insisted that I sing right then and there. I was quite intimidated, but good sense prevailed and I brought down the verse from the Quran and the Bukhari[11] containing the Hadith forbidding singing and [*Alhamdulillah*] thank God he backed off. He now supports my not singing anymore. See, if you use God's words, He always finds solutions for difficulties.

Thus, in this case it was the wife whose initiative influenced the husband. Suhaila felt that giving up music, and being able to convince her husband that she was doing the right thing, reflected deeper changes that affected the very constitution of her marriage. She narrates,

> One day I was singing in a gathering. I was wearing a white and red sari with bright red lipstick, my hair hanging loose on my shoulder. I know I looked like an angel. Then I began to sing, my favorite ragas, with a kind of passion that even the blind and deaf could sense. The men in the audience were neither blind, nor deaf. They were totally taking it in. And all the while I told myself that none of this was happening. After the (stunning) performance, a male guest came up to me and said, 'when you sang, the wind stopped blowing and the

> birds stopped chirping!' And my husband was there standing next to me and gloating. I told myself at the time that he was proud of me and showing me off. It's alright – a husband can and should be proud of his wife. But what should be the basis of this pride and showing off? Surely not another man's lust for his wife!!!? Where was the '*haya*' in my marriage? What was my husband doing to safeguard it? Is that the man he is supposed to be?

Haya is an Arabic word that can be found in several accounts of the cultivation of an Islamic disposition (Gole 2004; Mahmood 2005; Deeb 2006). Translated as modesty, the term is invoked when discussing comportment related to dressing and behaving and in contexts where women *have to* interact with men. Here I emphasize the 'have to' because the dominant thinking in these circles is that one must follow dictates from the Quran and *hadith* meticulously, and thereby minimize interaction with men. The evidence for Quranic dictate is verse 53, Sura Al-Ahzab, which asks the prophet's wives to take anything they need from unrelated men from behind a screen. This command is bolstered by verse 30 from Sura Nur, which asks women to lower their gaze and to not reveal their 'adornments' to anyone other than certain mentioned men. Both verses, in combination, are advocated as the commands that set the limits of modesty. While almost all the women studied agree that this dictate needs to be implemented with the practicalities of today's world in mind (such as work, co-education schools and universities, accepted modes of sociability), Suhaila's (amongst others') use of *haya* within marriage draws from the conventional sense in which the term is used to infuse new meaning to the marital unit. For example, in Suhaila's case, the understanding that women must follow certain conditions while interacting with men, and the recognition that in the context of her performance and the interaction with men that ensued, she was breaking the conditions, did more than compromise the modesty that should have characterized that particular interaction. The compromised modesty leading from a covert desire the man may have harbored towards Suhaila, in turn took away from the strength of the husband-wife relationship. Looking back, what outrages Suhaila was that her husband was participating in this 'sharing of his wife!' She says,

> How could we think that any of this was innocent. You know the *hadith* that says that when an unrelated man and woman are alone, the third present is always *shaitan* [Satan]. You see men do whatever makes them look and feel good. It is male arrogance and chauvinism that rules. And they get to choose – regardless of how it makes their wives look, regardless of what about their wife is being validated.

Suhaila's statement reveals quite a bit about how many marriages are constituted in the middle to upper classes, amongst which I conducted my research. In many of the lectures and discussions I attended, it was mentioned several times that marriages have become materialistic, shallow and devoid of the kind of love and affection that Islam lays out as ideal. In the mosque group, which consisted of mainly married women with young to adult children, the teacher spoke harshly about how wives these days 'demand, instigate husbands to accept bribes, and get caught up in the trimmings of the world (*duniya*).' The husbands, who were corrupt, in turn, indulged in the world in their own ways as well as through showering the wives with material goods. The result would be that wives would become 'trophy wives' – a show, and bearers of men's achievements. While most women contend that the wives become 'trophy wives' due to patriarchal pressures and expectations, the teachers call upon the women to take the power back into their hands, and change the rules of the game altogether. In other words, the women were called to reflect upon and change the foundations of their marriages, which was to begin by changing oneself and then converting their husbands into better Muslims and better men.

Suhaila drew great strength from the fact that she was the initiator of change in her marriage. She says,

> First I had to do the hard job of changing myself – leaving things that were dear to me, seeing the logic and reasoning behind new ways and doing things differently. Then I realized that unless my husband changes, it would be very difficult for me to lead an Islamic life. And so I began to work on my husband. But it had to be done very cleverly, without being too assertive, without making him feel that I was taking the power back, without rocking the boat – if you know what I mean. And the entire time I prayed – the countless times I woke up for *Tahajjud*.[12] And Allah answered my prayer.

Suhaila's husband's transformation is talked about by everyone that knows them. At one time known for his boisterous ways, his affinity for lively company and a good (alcoholic) drink, he now prays five times a day, has performed his Hajj and given up alcohol. In subsequent years, Suhaila assumed the role of a preacher. She gives Islamic talks in several places, and has even gone abroad to receive informal training from preachers. She says,

> My family is still most important, and with years of praying and persevering, my husband now believes and practices as I do. And it doesn't end there … He looks up to me with authority. The other day when someone asked him about a verse of the Quran, he said, 'Ask Suhaila'. Can you imagine that? I am so grateful to God.

Thus, Suhaila's journey from a beautiful singing socialite to a preacher and wife who feels in greater control of setting the rules is marked by a strife to overcome her own desires as well as a rethinking of how she as a woman was affecting herself as well as her marriage and others around her. The story encapsulated in the singing narrative addresses not only singing as an exclusive and solitary act, but the relationships in the larger world within which singing occurs.

Conclusion: the nation and its (un)singing women

In Bangladesh, understandings of womanhood have been subsumed by dominant development paradigms and initiatives that offer the promise of improving women's lives and representing modernity and progress for the nation. As Lara Deeb (2006: 30) writes, 'Measuring modern-ness by the "status of women" assumes a universal standard of measure, one that is based upon a particular liberal western feminist notion of emancipation and liberation'. The sidelining of insights into women's own sense of self has occurred at the privilege of an image of the woman en route to liberation, who participates in the labor force, frequents the cinema, and buys make-up (Feldman 2001: 222). The route to liberation, however, does not mark a linear trajectory. Charles Hirschkind and Saba Mahmood (2002) draw our attention to this non-linear pathway by critiquing the academic definitions of concepts of liberation and emancipation, which she argues are based on the premise of universal desire for women. They aim to redress the academic parochialism and write, 'We tend to forget that the particular set of desires, needs, hopes and pleasures that liberals and progressives embrace do not necessarily exhaust the possibilities of human flourishing' (Hirschkind and Mahmood 2002: 353). In the dominant constructs that have framed women's flourishing in Bangladesh, religion had not received a warm welcome. As pointed out earlier in the article, academic accounts, political debates, along with the popular imaginary have relegated a place for religion where Islam represents phenomena such as *fatwas* and Islamist terror attacks – phenomena denoting only that which is passive and oppressive for women.

The ethnographic section points out that becoming religious, for the women of the discussion circles, has had positive effects for women on two levels. The first area that has been touched upon is the inner self. In understanding the transformations of the inner self, the women's use of the term jihad is useful. As mentioned earlier in the chapter, jihad for these women does not mean armed battle. Rather, jihad is an inner struggle that involves deploying one's time, talents and energies in cultivating piety through obedience to textual edicts. For Arifa and Suhaila, the desire to obey what they believe to be God's words involves internal struggles, at the end of which they feel more humble and more modest, these virtues being attained through ego effacement. Arifa experiences and attains humility by realizing that her role in the home, and especially in relation to her in-laws, was excessive. The fact that she constantly strove to be a better cook, a better hostess, is now seen as acts of competition and therefore a source of mental and emotional turmoil. She now strives to discard her earlier domestic endeavors so that she may deploy her energies to attain closeness to God. Through that process, Arifa finds new self-awareness as well as a new understanding of her role and responsibilities within the home.

Suhaila's struggle to give up music leads her to think that she too has become more humble, by learning to live without praises, by 'taking away the I' from her life. In addition, she has altered the dynamics in her marital relationship, based upon a critical reflection on the past. She now feels that her marriage then, in sync with the expectations and socio-cultural standards of the wider society she belongs to, was materialistic and shallow. She argues that her relationship with her husband was shallow because it was based, among other things, upon others' validation of each other. She redresses the superficiality by putting a curtain between herself and other men, through the hijab as well as by not giving others access to her singing, thereby making her relationship with her husband a more direct and honest one. The women feel that the internal hardships they have had to endure in order to give up music have thus enabled them to better enact humility and modesty, ideals that allow them to validate their jihad, and reform inner selves towards greater piety.

Maimuna Huq writes that in the Jama'at, there is a particular gendering whereby jihad is explained as internal to the female members, whereas the men are urged to take jihad to the wider society. However, as Huq points out, the distinction between jihad against the self and jihad against society is artificial, as encapsulated in the jihad against the self is a broader address to socio-economic issues relevant to wider society (Huq 2009: 172). My examples of jihad also point out that in the internal battles women wage, they take on societal expectations, existing cultural norms and ways of living. Thus, Arifa's inner struggle speaks to the role of wife, daughter and sister-in-law – the roles in which women have been ascribed particular chores – the chores that women are then beholden to for recognition at home. Arifa's pursuit of piety by way of discarding music allows her to rethink those normative expectations and the tensions they underlie, thereby enabling a certain freedom from societal ideals. Suhaila's narrative of inner struggle similarly encapsulates a critique of the cultural expectations that frame the husband-wife relationship. Through these wider issues women's inner struggles are also addressed, the jihad against the *nafs* also becomes a jihad against society.

Just as singing women in the late 1960s were constructed, by the dominant narrative on nationalism, as agents of nationalist change, women such as Arifa and Suhaila, through discarding singing, become agents of change within their families as well as the wider society. The ethnographic cases presented here have highlighted the transformative potential that adherence to an Islamic position may offer. In light of the nature of transformations delineated, I ask: can we conceive of an Islamic agenda that encapsulates more than oppression and passivity for women? If, through engagement with religion and religious rhetoric, women feel more in control of their lives, do we place such a sense, even if it accompanies a certain social conservatism and the containment of sexuality, under the rubric of modernity and national progress? Are there grounds, then, to blur the sharp divide that separates religious rhetoric from liberal ones, especially as they both vie for modernity? Or, do we leave such transformations outside the purview of the modernizing nation, and keep Islamic dictates subsumed under retrogression and therefore in an undesired competition with modernity? Whether these transformations can be given a legitimate place within the discourse of modernity and that of a modern nation needs to be assessed through further analyses of what accompanies transformations brought on through religion, what the limits of those transformations are and who authorizes the discourse of change.

Notes

1. *Hamd* and *nath* are devotional songs about God and his messengers, notably the Prophet Muhammad. These songs are often aired on television especially during times of religious significance – Ramadan, the birthday of the prophet, etc. These songs are also sung in religious gatherings organized to commemorate auspicious or tragic events.
2. *Milads* are religious congregations organized around deaths, births or any other auspicious event, such as the construction of a new home, the launching of a new business, etc.
3. The language movement of 1952 marked the culmination of a contention felt by most Bengalis of East Pakistan, in reaction to Muhammad Ali Jinnah's declaration that only Urdu would be the state language of Pakistan. The protest by students, intellectuals and cultural activists was attacked by the Pakistani administration, leading to the arrest and death of several Bengalis. Bengali was granted the status of official language in 1962.
4. Author's translation.
5. *Chhayanaut* is the leading school for music in Bangladesh. It emerged at a critical time in history, when Bengali culture was being attacked by Pakistani authorities in a bid to suppress protests in East Pakistan that were geared towards the eventual struggle for the liberation of Bangladesh.
6. NGOs, especially during the BNP/Jama'at regimes, came under severe and even violent attacks from the Islamists where women attending NGO schools, receiving microcredit etc., were targeted and harassed by the local elite in collaboration with the religious leaders (Riaz 2004).
7. *Fatwas* are Islamic rulings given mostly against women for 'offenses' such as being involved in NGO activities and sexual transgressions.
8. Taslima Nasrine is a writer whose controversial writing questioning the tyranny of patriarchy harbored by religious parochialism led the Islamists to persecute her into exile (Alam 1998; Riaz 2009).
9. Wendy De Bano (2005) discusses musical performances in post-revolution Iran. In state-organized women-only musical festivals, women are offered a platform to express themselves through music. However, musicians often make a concerted effort not to overemphasize the sensual aspects of music. De Bano argues that outside of the context of state-sponsored and controlled events, musicians' bodily practices are intertwined with 'extra musical associations, including personal memories, historical phenomena and symbolic meanings' (De Bano 2005: 445).
10. *Jihad* here is used in the sense of a struggle with oneself to overcome desires and ways that are base and arise out of arrogance. This is considered by the women I studied to be the greatest form of *jihad* as opposed to the armed *jihad* in the battlefields. For a detailed discussion see Maimuna Huq (2009).
11. Bukhari is one of the two compilations of the sayings of the prophet Muhammad, and is considered to be the most authentic (*sahih*).
12. *Tahajjud* is a prayer that is to be performed in the middle part of the night.

References

Abu Lughod, Lila (1990) 'The romance of resistance: tracing transformations of power through Bedouin women', *American Ethnologist* 17(1): 41–55.

Ahmed, Rafiuddin (1994) 'Redefining Muslim identity in South Asia: the transformation of the Jama'at-i-Islami'. In Martin E. Marty and R. Scott Appleby (eds) *Accounting for Fundamentalisms: The Dynamic Character of Movements*, Chicago: University of Chicago Press, 669–705.

Alam, S.M. Shamsul (1998) 'Women in the era of modernity and Islamic fundamentalism: the case of Taslima Nasrin of Bangladesh', *Signs: Journal of Women in Culture and Society* 23(2): 429–461.

Banerjee, Sumanta (1989) 'Marginalization of women's popular culture in nineteenth century Bengal'. In Kumkum Sangari and Sudesh Vaid (eds) *Recasting Women: Essays in Colonial History*, New Delhi: Kali for Women, 127–179.

De Bano, Wendy S. (2005) 'Enveloping music in gender, nation, and Islam: women's music festivals in post-revolutionary Iran', *Iranian Studies* 38(3): 441–462.

Deeb, Lara (2006) *An Enchanted Modern: Gender and Public Piety in Shi'i Lebanon*, Princeton and Oxford: Princeton University Press.

Feldman, Shelley (2001) 'Gender and Islam in Bangladesh: metaphor and myth'. In Rafiuddin Ahmed (ed.) *Understanding the Bengali Muslims: Interpretive Essays*, New Delhi: Oxford University Press, 209–235.

Gardener, Katy (1998) 'Women and Islamic revivalism in a Bangladeshi community'. In Patricia Jeffery and Amrita Basu (eds) *Appropriating Gender*, New York and London: Routledge, 203–220.

Gole, Nilufer (2004) *The Forbidden Modern: Civilization and Veiling*, Ann Arbor, MI: University of Michigan Press.

Hirschkind, Charles and Mahmood, Saba (2002) 'Feminism, the Taliban and politics of counter insurgency', *Anthropological Quarterly* 75(2): 339–354.

Huq, Maimuna (2009) 'Talking Jihad and piety: reformist exertions among Islamist women in Bangladesh', *Journal of Anthropological Institute* (N.S.): S163–S182.

Jahan, Roushan (1995) 'Men in seclusion, women in public: Rokeya's dream and women's struggles in Bangladesh'. In Amrita Basu (ed.) *The Challenge of Local Feminisms: Women's Movements in Global Perspectives*, Boulder, CO: Westview Press, 87–108.

Kabeer, Naila (1991) 'The quest for national identity: women, Islam and the State of Bangladesh'. In Deniz Kandiyoti (ed.) *Women, Islam and the State*, London: Macmillan, 115–143.

Mahmood, Saba (2005) *The Politics of Piety: The Islamic Revival and the Feminist Subject*, Princeton, NJ: Princeton University Press.

Murshid, Gulam (2007) *Women, Religion, etc (Nari, Dhormo, Ittadi)*, Dhaka: Onnoprokash.

O'Connell, Joseph T. (2001) 'The Bengali Muslims and the state: secularism or humanity for Bangladesh?' In Rafiuddin Ahmed (ed.) *Understanding the Bengali Muslims: Interpretive Essays*, New Delhi: Oxford University Press, 179–207.

Riaz, Ali (2004) *God Willing: The Politics of Islamism in Bangladesh*, Lanham, MD: Rowman and Littlefield.

Riaz, Ali (ed.) (2009) *(Re)Reading Taslima Nasrin: Contexts, Contents and Construction*, Dhaka: Shrabon Publishers.

Siddiqi, Dina M. (2000) 'Miracle worker or womanmachine? Tracking (trans)national realities in Bangladeshi factories', *Economic and Political Weekly*, 27 May: L11–L17.

Siddiqi, Dina M. (2009) 'Taslima Nasrin and others: the contest over gender in Bangladesh'. In Ali Riaz (ed.) *(Re)Reading Taslima Nasrin: Contexts, Contents and Constructions*, Dhaka: Shrabon Publishers, 15–37.

Torab, Azam (1996) 'Piety as gendered agency: a study of Jalaseh ritual discourse in an urban neighborhood in Iran', *Journal of the Royal Anthropological Institute* 2(2): 235–252.

The visibility of a pious public

Rianne SUBIJANTO

ABSTRACT *The downfall of Suharto's regime in 1998 has been marked by the increasing visibility of Islamic piety in a form of popular culture. Tracing the emergent new genre of* sinetron religi *(religious TV series/serials), this paper analyzes the discourses of Islamic piety in several different series/serials, the construction of the public and the wider implication of these discourses for the position of Islam culturally and politically in Indonesia. This article argues that religious melodrama series/serials are a site of contestation of incoherent concepts of piety. As cultural texts, they interpellate their public and allow us to see how the visibility of religious discourses in public becomes a subject of negotiations and confrontations, while at the same time they trigger the politicization of piety as national identity.*

In the last few years, Indonesia's post-Suharto era has been marked by a proliferation of Islamic piety discourses in the media. Rock songs, melodrama series, movies, talk shows and youth magazines are among the media that are nuanced with Islamic features. Celebrities don veils; political elites adopt Islamic words in their language; natural disasters are interpreted as God's punishment; more veils in different fashions are visible in public spaces; Islamic satellite TV channels are launched; celebrity preachers with different approaches and styles are emerging; Muslim fashion stores are mushrooming. What do these tell us about religion and media in Indonesia as well as its public?

This paper aims to investigate how popular piety culture shapes and is shaped by its public. It focuses on several religious melodrama series and serials as case studies. The term 'series' here is used to refer to a specific form of TV melodrama. A series is a set of related programs or episodes. Each episode is self-contained. It has a beginning, middle and an end. For example, the series *Hidayah* (God's Guidance) consists of several related episodes, such as 'God's punishment to a whore' and 'A beautiful woman with a rotten heart'. Each story is completed within one single episode. When used in a plural form, the word 'series' refers to several TV series, each of which consists of several related yet independent episodes. On the other hand, unlike 'series,' a 'serial' is a fictional story that is divided into parts and broadcast daily or weekly. The story is ongoing; today's episode is a continuation of what happened yesterday.[1]

By treating melodrama series as a cultural space, I would like to ask: what are the kinds of Islamic piety contested through particular drama series/serials? How is the melodrama involved in (re-)shaping Islamic piety in the public? More importantly, what does it show us about the position of Islam culturally and politically in Indonesia within the intersection of modernity, secularism, and globalization?

I will start my discussion with a brief description of why popular piety culture proliferates in the country. I will continue by conceptualizing the theoretical underpinnings of the analysis. I then continue with a textual analysis of the melodrama series/serials. With the findings from this analysis, I investigate the debates and forms of piety in the public including the one that is in the level of political elites. In general, my argument is that religious melodrama series/serials are a site of contestation of incoherent concepts of piety. As cultural texts, they interpellate their public and allow us to see how religion in Indonesia is interpreted both through essentialist and non-essentialist points of view, making it a subject requiring both affirmation and modification.

Contextualizing the emergence of popular piety culture in Indonesia

In Indonesia, a country with a Muslim majority (which makes it the largest Muslim nation in the world), the State and political Islam are not so easy to disentangle. During Suharto's era, the Islamist movement and political groups were always politicized. Sometimes they were 'given' privilege[2]; most of the time they were repressed as they were seen as a threat to his national integration agenda.[3] Islamic symbols, such as veils, became visible in public years before Suharto left office in 1998, which was made possible because he needed to gain support from the Muslim community as his popularity started diminishing. However, the freedom to actually express religious piousness was totally consolidated after the downfall of the regime. Soon after, Indonesians witnessed an emergence of Islamist print and electronic media, Islamist political parties and Islamist non-governmental organizations. I would like to argue that after the downfall of Suharto's regime, Islamic revivalism in Indonesia could be seen in three different phases.[4]

The discussion of the position of Islam as the majority's religion in the nation-state emerged in the early decade of the reformation era.[5] Robert Hefner (2003) describes this epoch, saying, 'by these twin measures of intellectual vitality and mass base, Indonesia in the late 1990s was one of the most vibrant centers for new Muslim political thinking the modern world has seen' (Hefner 2003: 176). However, this did not last long because, as Hefner continues, 'their movement to create a civic-pluralist Muslim politics was quickly overtaken by events on the ground' (Hefner 2003: 176). While the first phase is characterized by the emergence of groups, parties and media with Islamic agendas and ideology mostly focused on the realm of nation building, the next phase, which is the period of 'the image of jihad and violent Islam', shows the sharpening fractionalization of these groups. This period was triggered by the ethnic conflicts in Maluku, in the eastern part of Indonesia, which was reported to be a conflict between Christians and Muslims (Spyer 2006). This epoch soon also coincided with the fallout of the 9/11 attacks and the subsequent American invasion of Iraq. However, as the local inter-religious conflict subsided, the face of Islam also gradually changed in the public stage. This is characterized by the emergence of popular piety culture in the media in a form of entertainment, which had started even during the conflict.

As might have also been the case in other countries, greater visibility of a non-violent pious Islam was seen in the 2000s. Internationally, the September 11, 2001 tragedy, the wars in Afghanistan and Iraq, as well as the worsening conflict in Israel and Palestine became the cause of the emergence of this visibility, either as an attempt to show religious solidarity (Scott 2005: 113) or to clarify and show 'the true face of Islam'. Locally, from 2004 onwards, Indonesia suffered from countless natural disasters, for example the tsunami that claimed over 220,000 dead and missing people, earthquakes, and landslides, among others. *Dzikir Akbar* (praying together) proliferated on TV channels, which sometimes showed the president and his staff taking part. The disasters were seen as God's punishment to the country with the world's most infamous record of corruption. People were seeking a solution by returning to God. Media corporations (or industry) saw the conditions as profitable and came up with popular Islamic presentations. The television screen was inundated with celebrity preachers, rock musicians singing a rock version of *Shalawat* (praises to Muhammad, the last messenger), and most importantly, religious melodrama series.

Conceptualizing popular piety culture and its public

Why popular piety culture?[6]

In this analysis, I will use the term 'popular piety culture' as a reference to the phenomenon in the third phase. While similar cases in other countries are usually named Islamification, Islamicization (Sreberny-Muhammedi and Mohammadi 1994) or Islamization, I avoid using those terms. With the stem 'Islam' attached to the morpheme '-ize' or '-fy', it implies not only an action to 'Islamize' or 'Islamify' done by a group of people – in this case, those to whom the authority belongs – but it also assumes that the very action is typically 'Islamic', which is problematic as Islam is interpreted differently in different cultures (Asad 2001). In the case of Indonesia, these terms are not suitable. First, what happens in the country is neither a top-down process nor a mere industry's exploitation of religion projected to gain consumers. Second, as the kinds of Islamist visibility are not coherent (as the analysis will show), I choose to avoid using the word 'Islam' since the very word itself usually demands an essentialist, Qur'anic interpretation, which might trap me into a normative understanding of the phenomena. I will, therefore, try to delve into it through the spectacle of cultural studies bearing in mind that as a form of cultural phenomena its very construction is contingent upon many aspects, including politics, culture, economy, tradition, and environment.

As a cultural form, I am interested to see how faith/belief is reified in the media and how that allows it to be visible in public. Therefore, I use the word 'popular' to imply its sense of visibility. Besides the sense of 'popular' that usually largely refers to 'market demand', I would also like to take the implication of the word further to interrogate what is visible/invisible, sayable/unsayable, and knowable/unknowable about public piety in Indonesia. This very sense of 'authority' attached to the domain of popular culture, such as songs, films, and melodrama, is what makes it crucial in the formation of the public's knowledge, behavior and religiosity nowadays.

Islamic piety in public

In understanding popular piety culture, it is important to understand it as a form of faith reification. By talking about these practices as reification of faith and not as religion, I prevent myself from being trapped into understanding it through the lens of Islam as an institution. This resonates with Smith's anxiety about the very use of the word 'religion' itself that refers to the highly essentialized and institutionalized notion. However, as Asad (2001) argues, in identifying religion, we need to delve into the materialities of religion, which constitute its form and being. It is thus important to pay serious attention to practices both religious and secular to account for the emerging piety culture in Indonesia. Secular in this case means 'an untidy historical complex that includes behavior, knowledge and sensibility in the flow of everyday life' (Asad 2001: 132).

Taking into account practices in understanding Islamic piety is important. This is because in Islam there is both embodiment and ensoulment. This means that faith should be expressed through bodily practices and being embedded sincerely in the soul in every aspect of a Muslim's life. It thus has 'structures of devotional practices, disciplines for cultivating religious virtues, and the evolution of moral sensibilities within changing historical circumstances' (Asad 2001: 142). This is because its defining features are both personal and communal. The latter implies the importance of the public in construing both personal and public piety. As religion is not the only aspect of one's life, secular aspects play a part in the complex dialectic of (re-)shaping what is an (un-)acceptable religious piety. This is why I take the concept of public seriously in understanding the practices of popular piety. Michael Warner's third sense of public, which is that it comes into being in relation to texts and their circulation (Warner 2002), will be used in this paper to understand how popular piety is created in relation to the products of media culture.

Sinetron religi as a site of contestation for piety culture

The first *sinetron religi* (religious melodrama series/serials) entitled *Rahasia Ilahi* (God's Secret) was televised in 2005. It soon gained a significant number of viewers. Because of its success, other channels started to copy the format. Within a short period of time, different kinds of *sinetron religi* mushroomed in Indonesia's private TV channels especially during prime time (7 p.m.–9 p.m.). According to ACNielsen research institution (Kurniawan and Ghozali 2007), their viewers were largely middle-lower class stay-at-home women – although in practice both male and female youth and adults also consume these shows. Debates in the media, blogs and TV interviews around the authenticity and validity of the religious messages in the series/serials and their accordance to Islamic teachings proliferated. Television thus becomes a cultural space in which different kinds of piousness are contested; it serves as a metaphor of the pious public.

Sinetron religi, as the name indicates, is a mixture of melodrama and parable.[7] As both are intended as a pedagogy of morality, the latter carries a special sense in that it relates God and humans, the heavenly and the earthly. Since the work of God is believed to be uncanny, the series through its melodramatic mode makes it accessible, *visually*. Through this visual experience what is sacred becomes profane and what is spiritual becomes materialized. God's supposed-to-be-mysterious work is embodied in a series of tragic events made through the lens of a video camera. Their portrayal centers on God's trial, reward and punishment.

The Qur'an – the holy book – and the Hadith – anything the Prophet Muhammad said, did or approved – tell about all aspects of a Muslim's life. Although they talk about rewards for virtuous deeds and punishment for the vice, they also talk about the importance of the process of complying with virtuous conduct. It tells about the rites of worship (*ibadat*) 'whose regular practice is necessary to the cultivation of the virtues and sensibilities required of a Muslim' (Asad 2001: 143). If the act of worship like performing the prayer (*salat)* is an embodied action of worshipping God, central to this is the 'ensoulment' of the act of worshipping itself, called 'the silent enunciation of one's intention (*niyya*)' (Asad 2001: 143). Other forms of ensoulment are virtuous fear of God (*taqwa*) and the virtue of *sabr* (endurance, perseverance, self-control) that can be practiced and embodied in different ways by different people. The practices of *taqwa, ikhlas* (to remain pure and faithful) and *sabr* are also considered forms of prayer, all of which requires *niyya* to attain the divine. While experiencing ensoulment is contingent upon the personal being, the practices of virtues as well as vice can be accessed as they are materialized, embodied through the corporeality. However, embodiment of virtues and vice is contingent upon other aspects that are worldly. It is bound to the norms, practices and cultures in a given society or place.

In *sinetron religi*, we will see how faith and piety are reified through televised symbols. The reification in this case goes through choices of plot, mis-en-scène and characterization that are typically 'Islamic' as well as through the aesthetics, or, borrowing Pinney's word, 'corpothetics'[8] of the ways the story is told through the lens of the camera to achieve the ends of the producers. The ends will be the make-believe of the story that is apparently only an interpretation of the words of the divine negotiated through the work and limitation of melodrama-making, the limits of the industry.

In general, the series/serials can be divided into five themes.[9] I am going to discuss each of the themes by giving an example from the episodes belonging to several series/serials. I will discuss the main focus of the story that depicts faith and piousness and analyze how it is reified. At the end, I will map the kinds of pious reification in the religious melodrama series/serials represented by these samples.

1. God's punishment to the sinner

The episodes with this theme are the pioneers of the religious melodrama genre. It was initiated by the series entitled *Rahasia Ilahi*, which was then copied by other production houses, who merely changed the content. However, the most popular religious TV series was *Hidayah* because it was aired on one of the most popular channels, Trans TV. As a TV melodrama series, every episode has a different story played sometimes by the same artists. Because the story centers on showing how God punishes a sinner, it is impossible to turn it into a 'serial', cutting the story into several episodes, as this will change the mood of the audience that has been built through its emotive and melodramatic tone. Since this is the focus, it is typical that the story will start with a dramatized depiction of God's punishment to the sinner as if giving the wrap-up before the story even starts. However, the plan is to appeal to the audience's emotion and to make them curious as to why he/she is considered a sinner and why such harsh and violent punishment is given to him/her. In the episodes with this theme, the part of God that is represented is the violent part.

For this analysis, I will take one episode as a sample. The title is 'God's punishment to a whore'. As mentioned, the scene starts with the conclusion of the story – the title itself.

> *A piano with a mysterious tone starts to play with gradually increasing volume. Darma enters the yard, smelling bad smells. He sees cats around and thinks that the cats are the source of the smell. The cats' quarreling along with the clash of cymbals builds suspense in the viewers' emotional attention.*
>
> *Darma enters the room.*
>
> Quick shot to the dead body lying on the bed covered with a Batik sheet (typically Indonesian way of covering dead body) [cymbals clash]
>
> Cut to Darma making uncomfortable expression because of the smell [zooming in, close up]
>
> Cut to Rina with head scarf crying [double zooming in, close-up]
>
> Cut to Darma [close-up]
>
> Wide shot of the room with the three people: Rina sitting next to the dead body; Darma standing next to it.
>
> Darma: Rina, why hasn't her body been buried yet? Where are the people in charge?
>
> Cut to Rina, still crying [close-up]: the people nearby don't want to help since her body smells bad and the form is weird. [cymbals clash]
>
> Quick cut to Darma, standing and looking at the dead body
>
> Quick cut to Rina [close-up]
>
> Quick cut to Darma [close-up]
>
> Cut to Rina, still crying and then shaking head (meaning refuse to answer) [extreme close-up]
>
> Cut to Darma, looking at the body again [close-up]
>
> Wide shot with the three of them
>
> Darma uncovers the dead body: *Bismillahirrahmanirrahim* [the sound of piano and clash of cymbals are interacting at a quick pace]

> The weird dead body is revealed [a loud clash of cymbals, the sound of piano becomes even louder]
>
> Ratna's dead body was lying on the bed, it has a dark brown face, eyes open and hands bent toward her chest.
>
> Wide shot to the three of them.

Here, the viewers' gaze is centered on the dead body, but the sensational experience is doubled – one is by seeing the weird dead body; the other is by sharing the emotion experienced by Darma and Rina through the aesthetics and facial expressions.

> Zoom in very quickly to the face of the dead body: eyes open and tongue poking out [cymbal clashing] [double close-up very quickly]
>
> *After uncovering the weird form of the body, Darma closes Ratna's eyes and mouth, unbends the two hands and folds them on her stomach. He continues uncovering the bent feet. The camera makes an extreme close-up to the blood under Ratna's body. Darma says* Astaghfirullahulazim *and unbends the feet. Finally, he covers the body with the sheet again.*
>
> *The sounds of cymbals and piano stop. Gradually they change into the melodramatic, soothing music of the quasi-religious theme song.*

This wrap-up scene, which is presented at the beginning of the story, is the most important part of the episode. It aims to create the mood of the audience and prepare them for what is to come. It is not an ordinary story. What they are about to 'witness' is God's work being visualized and accessed through their screen. As God's uncanny work is central to the theme, the mis-en-scène along with other features of aesthetics needs to support the making of God's mystery. The music is one of the most integral parts in constructing this. The crescendo of piano and cymbals clashing creates the dramatic atmosphere of the story, evoking suspense in the audience (Rajagopal 2001: 97). It complements the graphic description of God's punishment: the weird form of the body, the blood under the body assumed to be coming out of Ratna's vagina as her sin is of being a prostitute, and the bad smells evoked by the actions of the players and the language used. The intercut shots of Rina's and Darma's faces are used repetitively, elevating the emotion of the audience and enhancing the suspense. The deep and prolonged close-ups suggest the visual capture of emotions. Their focus is to let the audience experience the suspense and sensational feeling through the players' vivid facial expressions. But the suspense decreases as the scene ends and the song changes into the soft tone of the theme song that praises God. The use of the quick movement of the gaze, the marching tone of the piano and cymbals as well as the dramatizing properties, like blood, are utilized to create the suspense and thus elevate the mystery of God's work, but the slow movement of the gaze and the soft tone of the music and the scene ending with the two protagonists create a sense of anticlimax. The audience is left gasping after the suspenseful experience.

The story continues with the tale of a woman named Ratna who, in order to get money, kills her husband and leaves her mother and her son, and ends up being a sex worker. The plot is simple and typical with dramatic changes that happen within minutes. The scenes can be divided into two parts: those that portray Ratna, the antagonist character, and her vice, and those that depict the protagonists, her mother, her sister (Rina), and Ratna's friend (Darma). While Ratna is represented as being overwhelmed by the pleasures of the world – sex, money – her mother is shown as having full virtues of *sabr*. She wears a veil, and she always praises God, as do other protagonist characters. The dress and verbal code as well as behavior of the characters are clearly cut into two binary oppositions. Faith is reified through virtuous conduct, virtuous words, and the veil for women. Meanwhile, God's punishment that is materialized through the audio-visual description reveals what should remain a mystery via a simplistic, dramatic portrayal through the use of the typical mis-en-scène, plot and aesthetics.

There are two things that make the series problematic; that of the representation of God and that of the representation of women. As there are other things central to God, i.e. trial, punishment and rewards, the episodes of the series with this theme focus only on God's punishment. His trial, which is central to the making of punishment or reward, is not even depicted as such. From the beginning of the story the bad person is already bad, and the characterization of the bad person is typical, e.g. a whore, a gambler, an adulterous wife, a psychic etc. But, if we look at the titles, such as 'God's punishment to a whore' or 'A beautiful woman with a rotten heart', it is clear that women are very often characterized as bad and the wickedness is usually associated with them. While stereotypes are enhanced through the depiction of the good wearing veils and praising God, and the bad with their excessive wickedness, the end of each episode clearly stands as an expression of a pedagogy of morality, especially for women. While the women are moralized, their identities (and thus stereotypes) are reaffirmed, the good and the veil; the wicked and the sexy and the vulgar. Hidden in the representation is, thus, the old patriarchal ideology regulating women's bodies, masked in the name of religious reification.

2. *God's rewards to the believer*

The episodes of *sinetron religi* with this theme, like *Maha Kasih* (The Most Gracious), follow the framework of the previous theme. They center on the portrayal of the good and the bad. However, different from the previous theme, they focus on telling the story from the good person's point of view, which in the end will reveal how God rewards him/her. Therefore, while the mystery of God is exploited around the portrayal of woman's wickedness in the previous theme, in this set of stories God is represented as compassionate and gracious.

One example that I will use to ground this description is an episode entitled 'A Street Vendor Selling Fried Rice Becomes a Restaurant Manager'. The episode starts with the theme song with its slow music and lyrics containing prayers to God. It talks about a poor street vendor, Amir, who sells delicious fried rice because he is willing to spend more money to buy high-quality materials and ingredients. Because of this, he has a lot of customers, who abandon another vendor, Anton, whose rice does not taste as good as Amir's. This is where the conflict starts. In order to attract Amir's buyers, Anton devises many wicked plans, such as mixing kerosene with Amir's rice and breaking Amir's wheel cart. The conflict is raised through ironies. Amir, not knowing why, keeps *sabr* and *ikhlas* in facing the trial from God. In the end, because of his piousness in facing the trial, he wins. He wins through the help of an Islamic preacher, a figure who is always portrayed as the savior. Depicted in his typical dress, sarong, white T-shirt and a white hat, he only appears when the good is in conflict with the bad. His appearance is almost like a superman coming to save the world. Although he is not considered a sacred entity, religious lessons are usually explicitly directed to the viewers as the third person when he is in conversation with Amir. In the end, Amir wins by having Anton reveal the truth and by getting a place as a restaurant manager from a buyer who really likes his rice.

As in the case of the previous theme, this style of story is also simplistic. A good Muslim is shown to be over-*sabr* and over-virtuous and thus righteous. The Islamic preacher becomes the only symbol of virtue. Therefore, the expression of piousness is accessed through the use of statements praising God and the good deeds, which are the expressions of *sabr* and *ikhlas* in facing the trial, by the good party. Of course, his over-*sabr* and *ikhlas* are subject to contestation in that it shows the naivety of the good person. The use of cymbals clashing is heard but not as much as in the previous episode. It only appears when the scene is about the bad person doing bad things. With the lack of technological instruments, the episode unfolds through an exploitation of facial expressions. Any dramatic potential in the characters is pushed to the limit to create the effects wanted. This kind of theme is highly formatted in a way that virtue is portrayed through making a contrast with the existence of vice.

3. God's rewards to anybody with no conditions

While the previous two themes are set in a melodramatic tone, another set of drama series episodes offering a different theme uses the conventional aesthetics of film-making. There are no cymbals crashing or marching tones of piano or violin, no overuse of facial expressions, nor is there a mysterious work of God. The focus is not on building God's character but on the process through which the main character faces God's trial.

The story entitled 'A thief whose heart is stolen' is included in this theme. It is about a person named Wahyu who, together with his gang, likes to break into houses to steal money and other valuables. One day, when he is breaking into a Hajj's[10] house, he is caught. He is almost killed because the neighbors punch him, but the Hajj helps and rescues him. Since he is treated well by the Hajj, he repents his deeds. The story focuses on the process of his repentance and how he is tried because other people still treat him as a bad person and a thief. The whole neighborhood hates him, and he usually receives violent treatment from them. As a genre, the story is a mixture of action and devotion, facing the violent acts as a way to devote himself to God. In the climax of the story, he almost loses control by accepting to fight the people who are cruel to him, but he is saved unexpectedly by a friend.

As a non-melodramatic religious TV series, it offers a more real-life situation. There is no mysterious reward as such. The winner is the protagonist who wins the conflict with his enemies. The topic of the story is not uncanny as it is based on reality. It depicts how a person who has committed bad deeds can still receive rewards from God. In another set of episodes, very often the person who commits bad deeds is characterized as a veiled, wicked woman, challenging and opposing the view that a veiled woman is always a good person (Wardhana 2007).

Some religious symbols are still used, although not excessively, through the way the characters dress, talk and behave. Scenes of prayers are part of the way that religiosity is built in the story. The women wear veils. The Hajj always says wise words and praises God. Although in the beginning people might not realize that they are watching a religious series, by the end the appearance of a celebrity preacher strengthens this sense. After the story ends, the scene moves to a close-up shot of Arifin Ilham, the preacher. He starts by saying Islamic prayers and continues by discussing a verse from the Qur'an that the story reflects. He sits in front of a computer as if to show that he is not a typical traditional preacher. He is a modern preacher giving religious lessons through the use of film.

4. Contestation of Islamic teachings

Although there is only a few of them, the episodes with this theme are interesting in that they contest topics of Islamic teaching that are largely taken for granted. Among the themes that such episodes raise are polygamy, *mut'ah* marriage,[11] and the issue of transgendered people. These topics are usually talked about only in serious talk shows by authoritative guests. Similar to the making of other melodrama genres, the episodes in this genre build suspense through the use of typical melodramatic music, although not as excessively as in the making of the first theme. Conflicts are interwoven into the plot and in the obvious protagonist and antagonist relationship between the characters. In short, the story is still melodramatic in tone, but the content is unusual in that it attempts to raise critical awareness on the widely accepted concepts in Islamic teaching on polygamy or transgender.

The story entitled 'My female religious teacher is a man' contests the position of a transgendered person in the Islamic environment. It talks about the life of Bunda who is the female teacher who used to be a man. She is a religious teacher who owns an orphanage. The story tries to show the religiosity of Bunda by showing her praying to God in one of the scenes. Using wide shots from a neutral to a bird's eye angle, it tries to shift the audience's experience from seeing her praying from the spectacle of human being (in the neutral angle) to the spectacle of the Omniscient (in the bird's eye angle). The changes of the spectacle along with Bunda shown praying attempt to arouse the viewers' empathy. This is strengthened by seeing her wearing typical Muslim dress, veil and covering clothes.

The story is quite instructive in its pedagogy of morality. In one of the scenes, Bunda gives lessons on how to treat transgendered people.

Bunda [to the children in the orphanage]:	If you laugh at them, it is the same as laughing at Allah's (God's) creatures.
	...
Fitri:	Why are you always mad when somebody talks back at transgendered people?
Bunda:	Because I don't like discrimination.
Fitri:	But it is different, Bunda. They go against Allah's destiny.
Bunda:	You cannot judge before you prove it.

Despite being a transgender herself, Bunda's religiosity and piousness give her enough authority to be heard by the people. In another scene, the lecture is clear. Bunda asks a group of women to appreciate transgendered people. She says 'this is because Allah does not differentiate between men and women'. About the issue of transgender, she continues 'it is Allah's secret. They have the right to be directed to be a good (pious) person'. This explicitly criticizes general traditionalist preachers and religious teachers who see transgendered people as abnormal.

5. The use of Islamic teachings as the source of moral values

Kiamat Sudah Dekat (The End is Nigh) is a serial that can be included in this theme. The set of episodes is made by Deddy Mizwar, a famous and senior producer, as a reaction to the gory and bloody Islam represented by the other series. With his aim to make the film a counterargument and clarification of the piety expression made visible by the first and second themes, the plot, characterization, aesthetics and mis-en-scène give the story verisimilitude. The story does not center on God anymore. In fact, God's work is no longer materialized as such. It shows a story about the mundane, banal life of pious Muslims.

The story takes place in a lower-class area in Jakarta. It is about the life of a family comprising a father, a pious and religious teacher, and his young daughter, veiled and pious, living a modern yet religious life. Unlike other series that comprise different stories and are thus played by different characters and settings in each of its episodes, this serial follows the continuous story of this family and their neighbors. Everyday conflicts faced by the characters in the serial, such as platonic love, money, and school, are portrayed in a realistic manner. There is no over-use of Islamic words, or of scenes depicting prayers, or overuse of religious symbols. The veiled character, Zaskia, who plays the daughter is not only veiled in the drama but also in her real life. Some other characters do not wear veils because they do not do so in everyday life. Complete with humor, local Jakarta dialect (unlike the other series that sometimes use a very formal language, which is not in harmony with the everyday setting) and characterization played matter-of-factly, the serial offers a lifelike reflection of an everyday pious neighborhood along with its typical problems, and with no dramatization of the concept of 'bad' and 'good'. The message is therefore more wittily wrapped. It does not sound as instructive as the others, wrapped as they are in the aesthetics of typical melodrama and too overt and unrealistic characterization and mis-en-scène.

The discussion of the five themes shows us that religious melodrama series/serials have become a site of contestation where we see incoherent and sometimes contradictory concepts of piety. Some discussions focus on the way the aesthetics work to show the kind of piety shown; some others show the different themes and use of Islamic symbols that create their own concept of piety. They talk about God as well as interrogate gender positions in Islam, the meaning of Islamic attributes and how Islam is applied in everyday modern secular life. What does this incoherency tell us about piety in reality?

The interpellated public

What makes the screening of *sinetron religi* significant is that it has inspired public debate through mass media, religious preaching programs, gossip shows and even informal discussions, such as in the classroom, in the office or in a restaurant. People talk about it. Some compliment it; most others criticize it. Suddenly we are witnessing the visibility of a pious public, those interpellated by the series. The series creates its own public.

Most debates[12] are made within the rhetoric of the 'true Islam'. They criticize the authenticity of the Islamic content expressed by the series. One critic says that it is not enough to show a pious female character only by showing her in Muslim dress, praying punctually, honest and tough, yet having 'free' interaction with her male friends and expressing love in a non-Islamic way. Islam teaches the norms and ethics of male and female relationship. Sexual activities, for example, can only be performed within marriage. Therefore, activities that can lead to sex such as kissing, holding hands or hugging, should not be nurtured. Although men and women can be casual friends, having a boy–girl friend relationship has to be treated with caution as 'love and lust come in the same mask'. Usually, the relationship develops under the supervision of the parents. For the critics, it is not enough to show the pious character through the symbolic behavior and dress, but it is argued that a pious woman should be depicted as pious in totality. Even the actresses who play the characters are criticized because in everyday life most of them do not don a veil. Likewise, a veiled woman is expected to be good and not characterized as a bad person. Another critic defines a pious woman as sincere and modest in behavior. It is clear that a pious woman is expected not merely to express her piousness through dress and language but most importantly in behavior and through a vibrant sincerity, which reflects their total piousness. Putting non-veiled actresses in pious roles is therefore not appreciated: they are viewed as a 'chameleon' that changes colors. It is clear that the female characters in the series play the most pivotal role, and female bodies acquire a truly symbolic status, and it is their inclusion that creates a pious program.

Another critic criticizes the content as not being in line with religious teachings as they are nuanced with mystics, magic, and horrors, which are integral to some local cultures in the country. It says that mixing Islamic features, like the use of verses from the Qur'an to expel ghosts, mysticism and folktales is a humiliation to religion, especially Islam. Because of these series/serials, one critic says, Islam is now identified with ghosts and jins. Moreover, some critics criticize the scenes of domestic violence depicted in the series. They say that Islam is not violent.

For these kinds of shows, 'fundamentalists' question the validity of the teachings shown. They ask for strict censorship of these religious melodramas, as they will have the effect of downgrading Islamic teaching for the larger community. Religious preachers who support the programs are asked to evaluate themselves because their support will influence public opinion, in which religion is seen as teaching magical things that are not rational. For them, the label of 'piousness' carried is more appropriate for those programs that concentrate on themes such as strength, toughness and intelligence as they portray 'true' Islamic values. In short, they are expected to show true moral and Islamic values and not only use Islamic attributes, like the veil and the Qur'an, as a masquerade to show something more sensational, like mysticism.

As a reaction to this kind of series, a serial that has a more overt stress on piety can be discussed. For example, Deddy Mizwar, the producer of *Kiamat Sudah Dekat*, was worried to see the depraving effects of these kinds of series on the community's morality. He created a drama serial that later became the most popular, using verisimilitude and focusing on the application of Islamic teachings in everyday, mundane, banal life. This serial, focusing on the pious processes that help people face life's hardships, and Islamic values as moral everyday conduct, is highly appraised. It is considered educative and thus important for the community.

This serial produces a symbolic effect. An icon of an ideal young female Muslim is created. Zaskia, the main character in *Kiamat Sudah Dekat*, who dons a veil every day, both on and off camera, is one of them. In public, she represents herself just like in the drama, a modern, fashionable, pious, veiled young woman with sincere and polite behavior and language. She is seen as different from some other artists who don veils only as fashion, for example when they go to Hajj. Some others are afraid to play in this drama because they do not feel ready to plunge themselves into 'religious programs'. Tora Sudiro, a famous artist, says he is not ready because he does not perform his daily prayers regularly.

What does this debate show us about the public constituted by the circulation of this drama series/serial? First, it shows us that many of the critics, including the movement to counter the 'bad series/serials', are made within the conundrum of 'true Islam'. Despite its apparent grounding on an essentialist understanding of Islam, it does not show a strict definition of the Islamic system, as Smith argues (Asad 2001). This essentialist view questions the consistency and totality of piousness as shown both in behavior and dress, as well as ensouled through a sincere devotion to God. Second, when it enters the public domain, piousness no longer has the content of sacredness, of devotion to God. It becomes a relation between people, giving it as a sense of communality and common responsibility. What we notice here is that the pedagogy of morality does not actually work when the episodes are screened. People take the moral lessons through the public debates and reactions to it. At the same time, as the market demand changes, the discourse in the episodes is changed.

In understanding the concept of the pious public from this discussion, there are several defining premises that Warner (2002) maps which can help us. First, a public is self-organized and self-creating and thus should be seen as a space of discourse organized by the discourse itself. Therefore, in this sense, piety does not belong to institutionalized Islam as religion, but it is a product of a sense of belonging and activity organized by the ways discourses circulate. Second, a public is a relation among strangers. The texts that circulate, interpellate their public and ignite their performativity by participating in the public that the texts create. Therefore, the members of this public do not necessarily know each other (in fact, intimacy cannot create a public) (Warner 2002: 55–57). In the case of the religious melodramas, their appearance in the public through the media creates its own public and incites discussion and debates that follow the changes of the content of the texts that circulate. Because it is comprised of united strangers, the address of the public speech is both personal and impersonal. In the case of the pious public constructed by the series, the personal address is the use of religious words, symbols and dress. What makes it impersonal is the fact that it is not addressed specifically to a particular audience.

Next, the public is constituted through the mere attention that it pays to the melodramas. This implies the agency of the members of the public. This is expressed in the ways people start adopting symbols and attributes of Islamic piety in public spaces. A public is also the social space created by the reflexive circulation of discourse. This means that no single text can create a public. The pious public is not only created by the religious melodramas but also by other texts that create popular piety culture. The last premise is that the public acts historically according to the temporality of their circulation. The public as historical actors have an ongoing life maintained through the texts that circulate and that will continue to shape/re-shape the public. In the case of the melodrama series, they change the concept of piety along with the change of texts and debates that circulate in public space.

Through Warner's concept of public, the concept of piety as constructed through practices (or texts) helps us understand Asad's assertion that Islam is constructed as a set of practices that are contingent upon other non-religious aspects in addition to the religious ones. It helps us to refute Smith's essentialist view of Islam that it is highly systematized and thus is intolerant. Smith might conclude this from the case he followed in India, but the case in Indonesia shows us how the work of the public in a democratic setting in fact creates more tolerant religious practices that are – although systematized in that there are principles one needs to adhere to – also fluid in that they are subject to modification.

The symbolic piety

When *Kiamat Sudah Dekat* was screened, it was welcomed by many viewers, including religious preachers and community leaders. It is a good example of how a pious Muslim should be in everyday life. On 25 October 2005, Susilo Bambang Yudhoyono, the president, invited the whole production team, including the artists, to the presidential palace. He praised the team as having produced a good example of a TV program that morally educates the nation. His aim in praising the program is clear. It is to show that the program is in line with the government projection of national identity, civil and religious. This event does not only strengthen what is public about good Muslims, it also works as a symbolic capital for Yudhoyono's political platform. He takes advantage of the situation of growing public piousness.

If this decision sounds too premature, in the next event the president does give a much more significant proof. When an Indonesian religious movie entitled *Ayat-Ayat Cinta* was screened in the country's cinemas for the first time in post-Suharto Indonesian cinema history in 2008, it garnered three million viewers within a week, beating the previously most popular movie, *AADC*, in 1999. What makes it interesting is that Yudhoyono went to the cinema to watch the movie. This is something that has never happened before. However, what is even more significant is that he invited all the ambassadors and other political leaders in the country to watch the movie with him. The viewing practice thus cannot be seen as a personal activity. It becomes a national symbol consumed by the eyes of both the national community and the international representatives of Indonesia's identity. At the same time, Yudhoyono's symbolic capital, as a nationalist and religious figure, is created. This helped him on his way to the 2009 election.

Indeed, Indonesia has had a dual identity in the international stage for many years (Sukma 2003). But never before has it been reaffirmed through popular culture like this, where the impact ranges from the diplomatic to the local, national and international public at the same time. It is also an arena where an identity of a public is created through circulation of texts. Although we do not know which one comes first, a kind of chicken-and-egg mode, Yudhoyono's pious visibility seems to be a move toward a projection of a pious public, in this case the nation, which the work of the market and industry helps to set up. This affirms Derrida's (1996) statement of religion becoming a medium of national mobilization. As Warner (2002: 77) argues, 'the projection of a public is a new, creative and distinctively modern mode of power'. So far, Yudhoyono has been successful in doing this.

Conclusion

Popular piety culture is the product of the sociocultural situation in Indonesia where the work of the media industry made visible what used to be taken for granted. Religious melodrama series have become a site of contestation in which popular piety culture is constructed and reconstructed, making the pious public visible through the process of its circulation. Meanwhile, at the political level, this becomes reified to the status of a national culture through the symbolic act of the president who took advantage of the emergence of popular piety culture to reaffirm its construction, making it even more prominent in the process. Therefore, although television does not 'manage' the people, by putting images of popular piety culture it creates its public, which allows us to see piousness as a social construction. The process of its construction is fluid and interacts dialectically between the concept of Islam that requires both affirmation and modification with the concept of modernity and secularism.

The title of this paper thus works metaphorically in three ways. First, it asserts the visibility of a pious public represented and contested through the religious melodramas. Second, it refers to the pious public created by the circulation of the series/serials that then (re-)constructs the episodes within the series as well as the concept of piety. Third, it accounts for the symbolic act of the president that affirms the existence of a pious public in Indonesia. In fact, it makes it a national identity that is rendered visible before the eyes of the national and international audience. Indeed, cultural and political Islam in Indonesia has a different face than the general representation of Islam in that it is constructed within the intersection of the need to accommodate the different religions, modern and secular life, local culture, global representation of Islam, and the Muslim majority themselves.

Notes

1. The term *'sinetron religi'* in Indonesian language refers to both religious TV/melodrama series and serials.
2. Backed by the CIA, Suharto came to power through a coup against the first president, Sukarno, who was accused of supporting communism in the country. Suharto gained support from Islamist organizations and the Muslim community through propagandist ideology, saying that communism was anti-Islam.
3. Conflicts of interest had existed before the country had agreed to become a nation, especially from some parts of the Muslim community who wanted to construct the state based on Islamic Shariah. The first article in the Jakarta Charter mentioning that Indonesia was to use Islamic Shariah was annulled after a long discussion by the founding fathers, who realized this would not be able to accommodate Indonesians who were not Muslims. In 1948, Darul Islam, an organization built with the idea to build Negara Islam Indonesia (NII) (Indonesia Islamic State), was established and led by Kartosuwiryo. Since then, this so-called 'militant Islamic' was seen as a threat to the existence of the country.
4. Indeed, this is not an attempt to simplify what might be a more complex situation; therefore, it is also important to bear in mind that one phase might coincide with another. This means that it is not a clear cut division or timetable.
5. After the downfall of Suharto, Indonesia is seen to enter the *'era reformasi'* (reformation era).
6. This term is inspired by Saba Mahmood's *Politics of Piety* (2005). However, different from the women's piety movement in Egypt's mosques she discusses in that book, the concept of piety in this article is based on its visibility on the ephemeral, secular medium and products.
7. I am aware of the biblical sense of this term. I am borrowing it to give a sense of the unworldly root of the story as opposed to the use of the word 'story'.
8. Pinney makes an important argument in approaches to visual studies. He develops 'a critique of conventional approaches to aesthetics and argue for the notion of "corpothetics" – embodied, corporeal aesthetics – as opposed to "disinterested" representation [e.g. aesthetics]... The relevant question then becomes not how images "look", but what they can "do"' (Pinney 2004: 8).

9. This is based on my interview with Veven sp Wardhana, a senior researcher on mass media in Indonesia.
10. Hajj is a title given to people who have gone to Mecca for a pilgrimage. In Indonesia, people who get this title are usually highly praised and are expected to behave in compliance with religious norms and ethics.
11. Or *nikah mut'ah* is generally seen as a type of marriage, similar to a permanent marriage (*nikah*), which makes the relationship *halal* (or Islamically acceptable). However, the marriage is temporary according to Islamic law and is dissolved after the fixed time has expired. This type of marriage is highly disputed. Some regard it as an acceptable form of marriage, but others deem it to be un-Islamic.
12. The debates are traced from newspaper articles, magazine articles, blogs and the writer's experiences of conversing with different groups of people.

References

Asad, Talal (2001) 'Reading a modern classic: W. C. Smith's "The meaning and end of religion"', *History of Religions* 40(3): 205–222.

Derrida, Jacques (1996) 'Faith and knowledge: the two sources of "religion" at the limits of reason alone'. In Jacques Derrida and Gianni Vattimo (eds) *Religion: Cultural Memory in the Present*, Stanford, CA: Stanford University Press, 1–78.

Hefner, Robert W. (2003) 'Civic pluralism denied? The new media and *Jihadi* violence in Indonesia'. In Dale F. Eickelman and Jon W. Anderson (eds) *New Media in the Muslim World: The Emerging Public Sphere*, Bloomington: Indiana University Press, 158–179.

Kurniawan, Sigit and Ghozali, Anang (2007) 'TV program trend 2008: the number of TV programs for children increases; religious melodrama serials flourish' 'Tren Program TV 2008: Program Anak Naik, Sinetron religi Marak', *Marketing Magazine*, 12, http://www.marketing.co.id, accessed 26 April 2008.

Mahmood, Saba (2005) *Politics of Piety: The Islamic Revival and the Feminist Subject*, Princeton: Princeton University Press.

Pinney, Christopher (2004) *'Photos of the Gods': The Printed Image and Political Struggle in India*, London: Reaktion Books Ltd.

Rajagopal, Arvind (2001) *Politics After Television: Hindu Nationalism and the Reshaping of the Public in India*, New York: Cambridge University Press.

Scott, Joan W. (2005) 'Symptomatic politics: the banning of Islamic head scarves in French public schools', *French Politics, Culture & Society* 23(3): 106–127.

Spyer, Patricia (2006) 'Media and violence in an age of transparency: journalistic writing on war-torn Maluku'. In Birgit Meyer and Annelies Moors (eds) *Religion, Media and the Public Sphere*, Bloomington: Indiana University Press, 152–165.

Sreberny-Mohammadi, Annabelle and Mohammadi, Ali (1994) *Small Media, Big Revolution: Communication, Culture, and the Iranian Revolution*, London: University of Minnesota Press.

Sukma, Rizal (2003) *Islam in Indonesian Foreign Policy*, London: RoutledgeCurzon.

Wardhana, Veven Sp. (2007) 'Television and fashionista or contemptible women' 'Televisi dan Fashionista atawa Perempuan Nista', *Woman Journal* (*Perempuan*) 54: 39–49.

Warner, Michael (2002) 'Publics and counterpublics', *Public Culture* 14(1): 49–90.

Women, Islam and nation in Bengal

Firdous AZIM

The new scholarship on Islam and Muslim societies is manifested in a plethora of books and writings, and driven by a need and wish to examine the structures that determine academic understanding of social and religious factors. The urgency of this project has of course accelerated after the events of September 2001 and the decade-long War on Terror.

In South Asia, this has meant re-examining, at one level, the 1947 partition, and the ways that the movement of peoples affected the nation-making efforts in India and Pakistan. In this context, Bangladesh has often taken a back seat, as a country that defines itself as a nation that came into being not as part of that post-colonial moment, but a quarter of a century later, in 1971. Bangladesh's coming-into-being is traced to its struggles against the Pakistani state, which is typically seen as part of an assertion of a Bengali identity, in contradistinction to a Muslim one, which pertains to being Pakistani. The denial of the primacy of a Muslim identity is celebrated in Bangladesh history as part of an assertion of Bengali modernity – Pakistan being seen as Islamic and hence atavistic, and the emerging Bengali as secular and modern.

What gets lost in this version is the 'Pakistan' period of Bangladesh's national history, and the ways in which Bengali Muslims had sought to insert themselves into a Muslim polity. It also overlooks the effects that the 1947 partition had in Bengal, and what the movements of peoples may have meant to those engaged in migration, as well as the economic and social effects that this division must have had. Nearly four decades after, we are in a position to examine a forgotten history, and to look anew at what being Bengali may mean in Bangladesh.

Reviewing histories of partition and post-colonial nation-making is useful in that it also helps to look afresh at South Asian nations and their relations to each other. Also looking at the status of Islam in political life today throws light not only on the resurgence of Islam in politics, but also to examine the way in which the struggle for the separation of Bangladesh from Pakistan had been formulated. Looking at Islam and politics and the politics of being Muslim in Bangladesh is therefore interesting from many perspectives: from the cultural and political history of South Asia, a remapping of the national history of Bangladesh, and from looking at a resurgence of Islam and politics that shares some of the same concerns as in other nations, but which brings – because of the peculiarities of its own history and positioning – new dimensions to our understanding of this modern-day phenomenon.

The books I have chosen to review concentrate not on the construction of Islam or a Muslim polity alone, but on the position of women within emerging structures. This emphasis on women is of course not fortuitous, as we know that the status of women in Islam has been a problematic one and a matter of debate since colonial times. The nationalist resolution of the woman question (as Partha Chatterjee would have it) left the Muslim woman outside its purview. Not only in its colonial rendering, but even in the Bengali nationalist understanding of women's position, the Bengali woman is pitted against the Muslim, the former being the ideal representative of the modern nation. In this context, the growing number of veiled women, or women wearing headscarves and other items of 'Islamic' attire have elicited alarm and are seen as part of the growing Islamicisation of society. The veiled woman is read as a sign of rejection of the Bengali aspect of national identity, but can equally be seen as a merging of the Muslim with the Bengali. Women, veiled or otherwise, form part of a national cultural debate.

This article will review the two books and examine their contribution to this ongoing debate. Before doing that, it will be useful to recount that language has been seen as the fulcrum on which Bengali identity rests. Histories of Bangladesh look at the way that Bengali, in its various forms, has formed the crux of the struggle for independent nationhood.[1] On the other hand, most studies of women in Bangladesh have come out of the development discourse, and it is only recently that a spate of books on women has helped to change the main features of the discourse, showing how women are placed in our understanding of national culture. A pioneering book in this regard is Sonia Nishat Amin's *The World of Muslim Women in Colonial Bengal: 1876–1939* (1996). Other books include Taj Hashemi's *Women and Islam in Bangladesh: Beyond Subjection and Tyranny* (2000), or Maimuna Huq's *New Media in the Muslim World: The Emerging Public Sphere* (2003). Amin's book draws the main contours of the discourses amongst which the Bengali Muslim woman acquired a public presence in the late 19th and early 20th century, thus setting the stage for historical work. Maimuna Huq, on the other hand, looks at the contemporary literary and media influences on women, especially with the advent of what she calls the Islamic romance tale. Hence, some light is being shed on the cultural lives of women, as well as examining the meaning of the cultural centrality of women in the process of national development.

It is in this context that the books under review gain significance and merit great attention. To begin with: Mahua Sarkar's *Invisible Histories, Disappearing Women: Producing Muslim Womanhood in Late Colonial Bengal* (2008) looks at the silence or absence of Muslim women even in feminist writings on Bengal. Feminist re-readings of Bengali nationhood look at the history as it pertains to Hindu women, beginning from the reform movements of the early and mid-19th century, to the emergence of women as writers and the gradual entry of women in the various professions.[2] The Muslim woman, even when she does enter this story, is often present as an exception. The writings and works of Rokeya Sakhawat Hossain occupy this exceptional status, and because she is one of the most radical writers of her times, her works are read in isolation and not put into the context of other women's writing. Mohua Sarkar's book does a wonderful job of exploring the ways in which the Bengali Muslim women entered the public sphere in the early part of the 20th century, examining a host of journals and magazines that formed the platform where the hitherto neglected Muslim population expressed its concerns, and debated issues pertaining to nationalism and modernity. The Bengali Muslim, Sarkar contends, had remained largely outside the purview of the mid-19th century renaissance, which had concentrated on the emerging Hindu middle and professional classes. With the publication of W.W. Hunter's *The Indian Musulmans* in 1872, it became apparent that Muslims were in a majority in the province of Bengal. Hunter's survey had also divided the Bengali Muslim into two classes, the *ashraf* and *atrap*, which worked as both a class and racial division, the former being part of the Muslims who had come to India as conquerors and rulers, and the latter being composed of converts mainly, it is said, from low-caste Hindu communities. The *ashraf* were identified as part of the old Muslim ruling aristocracy, often speaking Urdu, and different from the Bengali-speaking peasant converts. The 'new' Muslims, who began to make their presence felt in writing, literature and politics at the end of the 19th and the beginning of the 20th century, seek to go beyond these class divides, and take their place within the debates on nation, modernity and secularism that mark this era.

Mohua Sarkar explores how the 'woman' question enters this discourse, both from the pens of women writing, but as part of the larger debate on nationalism and modernity. This part of the book performs a valuable historical task, bringing to light newspapers, journals and publications. The debate, however, is always framed within the binaries of tradition and modernity, and women's ambiguous positioning within it. This binary seems often to express itself through the ways in which 'Muslim' is expressed in contradistinction to 'Hindu', and thus the divide remains intact, with the difference that a Muslim presence, instead of being ignored, is recorded. 'Negotiating Modernity' (the title of the third chapter of the book) for Muslims meant trying to break the binaries of class race and language that Hunter had placed them within. Also, and interestingly, the struggle for nation had to be forged not only against the colonial rulers, but involved a process of differentiation between Hindus and the Muslim community. How this difference was negotiated remains unclear, as the original contention of the book is that Muslims remain invisible in what Sarkar considers to be mainstream discourse.

The most interesting and longest section of the book is Chapter 4, recording a 'Difference in Memory'. Based on in-depth interviews with middle-class Bengali Muslim women born between 1910 and 1950 and who now live either in Dhaka or Kolkata, Sarkar sees how Hindu–Muslim relationships were experienced by urban middle-class women. A set of interviews with Bengali Hindu women of the same age displays a difference, showing that the same set of events is relived in memory from different perspectives. In the interviews, there seems to be, on the part of the Muslim women, attempts to present themselves as people who are, and have been, completely at ease with their Hindu sisters, effacing the differences that are revealed even as they speak. Women whose families chose to remain in Kolkata, not migrating to the then East Pakistan, seem to be more adamant about asserting their ease with Hindus, but that is also the case with the women who had migrated. Partition had been experienced by these women as something that had been decided elsewhere, as even the decision to migrate had been made by elder, often male, family members. Another 'difficult' memory that stands out is of the 1946 riots. Migration to Dhaka had meant for many of these women giving up the rich cultural and social life that they had enjoyed in Kolkata, but there was also a recounting of the ways in which they had settled in the new country and city.

The book is based on women's first-person voices – as written in the first half of the 20th century, and recounting their memories in contemporary times. Together they form a rich mosaic of the experiences of Partition, of the debates on Muslim nationhood and the place of women within it, throwing fresh and new light on the construction of a new nation. However the absolute concentration on Bengal limits the book, as the debate on Muslim modernity and nationhood was animating the nationalist discourse all across India. Placing these debates within the wider Indian framework would have added to the richness of the book. In addition, debates on modernity, Islam and women have been part of the anti-colonial discourse in many countries, such as Egypt, Turkey or Iran. Many of the journals that Sarkar has referred to had articles on reforms in these Middle Eastern countries, as well as on what was happening in Indonesia at that time. While the book does not provide the wider framework, it opens up ways in which comparative studies could take place, and further research conducted on women, Islam and modernity.

The second book under review, Elora Shehabuddin's *Reshaping the Holy: Democracy, Development and Muslim Women in Bangladesh*, also published in 2008, looks at the status of women in contemporary Bangladesh. Women continue to be at the centre of development initiatives, and the new status that women have come to occupy has become a matter of much contention within the body politic. Shehabuddin traces how women are seen, in the political process, as a separate constituency that needs to be addressed. The modernization policies and programs of both the government and the state have often pitched the 'new' woman against the traditional. Interestingly, the 'modern', in the new construct, is not shown to be inimical to the traditional, but as somehow forming a continuum between the two. For example, micro-credit programs encourage home-based enterprise, thus making the woman a *grihalakshmi* (or the angel in the house) in new and dynamic ways. Shehabuddin's research shows how Islamicist politics has dealt with these new spheres that are opening up for women, and how women in turn negotiate these new spaces. The chapter entitled 'Contesting development' traces the contests and the compromises. For example, on the vexed question of the veil and purdah: development efforts have been shown as encouraging women to violate these religious and social norms. NGOs have been characterized as 'Trojan horses' through which 'Western imperialists' attack local culture, education and religion (Shehabuddin 2008: 124). These critiques of NGO and development activity are not limited to Islamist groups alone, but are often voiced by the Left as well. However, a head-on collision has taken place only between development and Islamist groups, especially with attacks on NGO schools during the mid-1990s.

Women's employment has also been a bone of contention. Women form the large bulk of the workforce in garments factories, and despite the abysmal conditions of work, this factory employment has provided, for the women involved in the work, a great source of empowerment (Kabeer 2001). While these are contested terrains, Shehabuddin demonstrates that it is 'different understandings of development and modernity [that] coexist in rural Bangladesh today' (Shehabuddin 2008: 151) that bring about these conflicts. Islam has its own version of modernity, she asserts, that does not necessarily gel with the World Bank and donor-funded development programs followed by NGOs. The Jamaat-i-Islami, as the leading Islamist party in the country, offers its own version of gender roles and paths to women's empowerment, which spelt out in its various documents, including its election manifestoes. Poor rural women – the target of development – thus have a choice, and Shehabuddin explores the choices that women are presented with.

One of the choices, in the kind of electoral democracy that is being practiced in Bangladesh over the last two decades, is the political or electoral choice. In the last two elections – in 1996 and 2001, in the case of Shehabuddin's research – women, even those who practice religion, do not report voting for religious parties. The book ends with a four-page 'Coda', which tries to map out the choices that women have in front of them, and in exercising that choice, women seem to be developing an agency. Negotiating between difficult terrains, choosing between economic and social alternatives, the Muslim woman in Bangladesh has indeed come a long way.

The nexus between Islam and politics is problematic for the countries of South Asia. Secular thinking tends to ignore these connections, but South Asia itself is defined by states whose borders were drawn as a result of an assertion of Muslim identity, and which are, at the moment, involved in new challenges with which that identity is faced. Women have always been central to the process of national identity formation, and in the contests and contradictions with which such monolithic identity making is, of necessity, faced. It is hoped that the new scholarship will open up new ways of negotiating contested terrains, and will shed new light on the historical and cultural positioning of women in this process.

Notes

1. Cf. Anissuzaman (1969) or Ahmed (1988).
2. Cf. Akhter and Bhowmik (1998).

References

Ahmed, Rafiuddin (1988) *The Bengal Muslims, 1876–1906: The Quest for Identity*, New Delhi: Oxford University Press.

Akhter, Shaheen and Bhowmik, Moushumi (eds) (1998) *Women in Concert: An Anthology of Bengali*

Muslim Women's Writing, 1904–1938, Kolkata: Stree.

Amin, Sonia Nishat (1996) *The World of Muslim Women in Colonial Bengal: 1876–1939,* Leiden: Brill.

Anissuzaman (1969) *The Muslim Mind and Bengali Literature (Muslim Manosh O Bangla Sahitya, 1757–1918),* Dhaka: Bangla Academy Press.

Hashemi, Taj (2000) *Women and Islam in Bangladesh: Beyond Subjection and Tyranny,* New York: St. Martin's Press.

Huq, Maimuna (2003) *New Media in the Muslim World: The Emerging Public Sphere,* Bloomington: Indiana University Press.

Kabeer, Naila (2001) *The Power to Choose: Bangladeshi Women Workers and Labour Market Decisions,* Dhaka: The University Press Limited.

Sarkar, Mahua (2008) *Visible Histories, Disappearing Women: Producing Muslim Womanhood in Late Colonial Bengal,* Durham and London: Duke University Press.

Shehabuddin, Elora (2008) *Reshaping the Holy: Democracy, Development and Muslim Women in Bangladesh,* New York: Columbia University Press.

Popular expressions and matters of faith

Safia AZIM

Walking down the streets of Dhaka – or anywhere in Bangladesh for that matter – popular expressions of matters of faith, specifically Islam, strike the eye. Painted on public transport vehicles such as trucks, three-wheeled auto taxis or bicycle rickshaws, inscribed on walls and minarets of mosques, paintings and calligraphy dot the landscape. While Islamic expressions are normally associated with high art forms that reflect deep spirituality and faith, or more recently with the growing politicization which is often seen as extremism or fanaticism, these popular images reflect an everyday and comfortable coexistence with the faith. Eschewing the high art forms of the Mughal and Sultanate traditions of the 15th to the 18th centuries, these images reflect a more folk tradition, and an easy accommodation with religion and culture. Contemporaneously, they add kitschy cinematic styles, associating it with pop art and culture.

Two years of taking random photographs of various features of the Bangladeshi landscape led to this collection of images, which bring to focus the connection between pop art forms and expressions of faith in Bangladesh. Vehicular art has been documented quite extensively in South Asia, including Bangladesh. The following photo essay seeks to highlight matters of faith in street art forms, which includes the vehicular.

Windows of faith

These mosque windows, simple as they are, reflect three sources of influence. The one of the left combines the typical Islamic iconography of a crescent and star with colours (green, red and gold) that are totally folk Bengali, including the manner in which the wood planks (in turquoise) are placed on the window. This cultural hybridty is also visible in the windows on the right. The variety of influences ranging from the Magreb (top right) to the European grille pattern on the bottom show the multifarious ways in which mosques' architecture has evolved.

Towers of Faith

The minaret, a staple feature of mosque architecture, undergoes many permutations, and depending on the economic prosperity of the area, soars high above the horizon, or makes a little dent. This is the most decorated and ostentatious feature in mosques. However, the famous mosques in Bangladesh concentrate more on the dome, making the minaret a more popular expression.

Mosques

All around Bangladesh, from urban street corners and rural pathways, the mosque is a ubiquitous structure. It is seen as reflective of the prosperity of an area, and performs multiples roles as a community centre, Quran reading classes, and a place for men to congregate. Even in the most crowded of areas they stand out as beacons of peace and serenity, a sanctuary for the local people.

From a still to a moving canvas

From architecture to art, popular expressions testify to human aesthetic need. Our street artists are paid a minimum wage for the work they put into beautifying a vehicle. Ultimately what we are seeing is a labour of love, in every small detail of the embellishments which adorn a rickshaw or a lorry. Let us start by looking at the many ways in which the creator is named. In this collage of the word 'Allah' in the Arabic script we also see a transformation of classical Arabic calligraphy to Bengali folk forms.

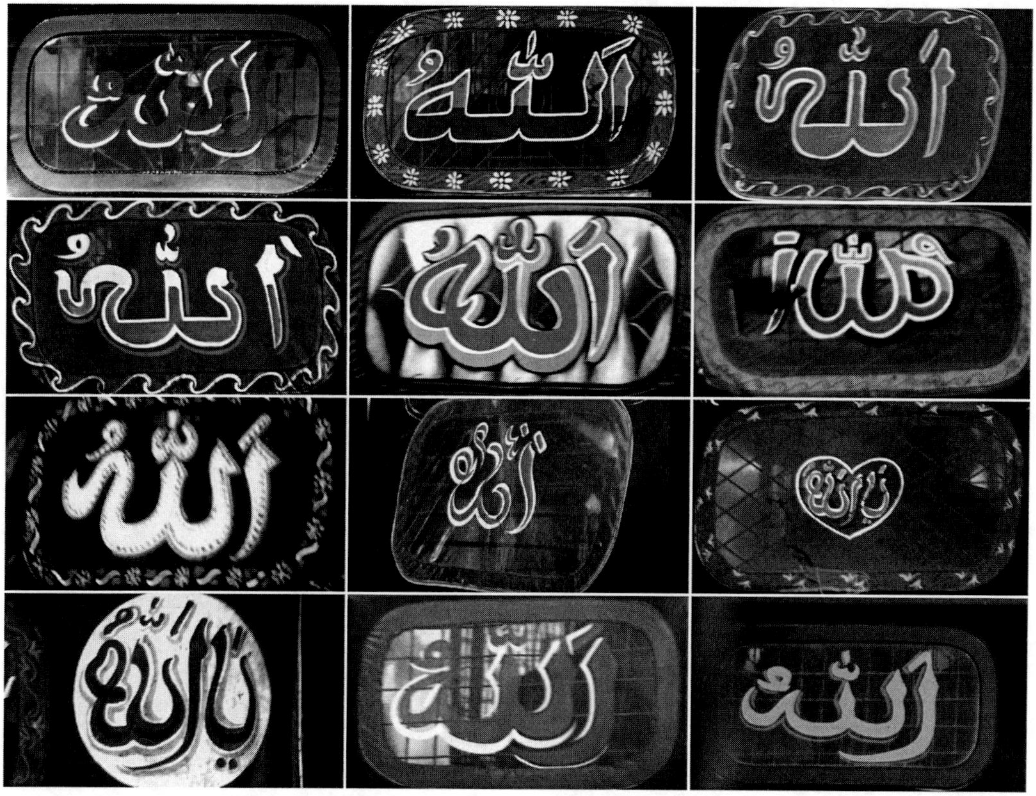

The colours, combining reds, yellows, and greens are redolent of Bengali styles, as these are the colours that are seen in our weaves, on pottery and painted woodwork. The calligraphy also shows a lack of sophistication and, in one of the pictures, actually appears as a mirror image of the Arabic Allah. Although using the Arabic script and word, this is a universally recognized symbol all over the Islamic world. However, this art form goes far beyond Islamic precepts, as the word Allah written on the breast of a Brahminy kite shows. In the popular sphere, Islam becomes a truly syncretic religion.

The many forms that the word Allah takes and the many combinations in which this symbol appears are seen in the hoods of the following lorries; Allah is coupled with Mohammad in Arabic script, and they flank images of the Kaaba in Mecca and the praying boy, who is discussed in more detail later.

Preaching Islam

Syncretic or not, popular expressions do proselytize, and are perhaps even more effective in spreading the word and enforcing the practice than preaching from the mosque. From the written word to images, the following pictures act as a call to piety. The messages in the Bengali script call on the faithful to perform *namaz*, to fast in the month of Ramadan, to give alms to the poor and to fear Allah. They also express a faith in Allah's protection and grace.

From words to images, the boys in the following pictures embody the image of piety and virtue that is supposed to be ideally Islamic. Interestingly, the boys are shown in what is considered appropriate 'mosque' attire, and hark back to a South Asian Islamic heritage. Although Bengali in feature, they are made to merge with a larger Muslim polity or *ummah*. The image also reflects popular male perceptions of male beauty.

From the boy to the mother

For the Bengali, one of the favorite sayings from the Quran is that heaven lies under the feet of the mother. Mother-worship is part of Bengali culture, with the nation and language being equated with the mother. So the boy is associated with the mother, and women enter this popular religious iconography through their young sons.

The idealization of the boy also involves the mother, and the beauty of the boy is echoed in his mother's features. But a beautiful woman has also to be pious, and pictures of the praying woman (cleavage notwithstanding) are commonly seen. The praying woman seems to be praying for her son, or the country. The woman in this picture is flanked by other folk images, such as the tiger, the name of the rickshaw owner, and the emblematic Allah.

Images run amok, and the following image seems to straddle popular cinematic themes and religious imagery. The man in the middle is obviously a *moulvi* (Islamic preacher) torn between two women, who may well be his older and younger wives. While a plurality of wives is permitted to him, the three faces display anguish and pain, and seem to be playing out a typical triangular drama in their lives.

When Islam hits the streets and takes on popular forms, it vies for attention with all kinds of other images. Within that, our artists carve out pictures and forms that they feel will have an appeal, and reflect their engagement with matters of faith and relate it to daily lives.

Index

Abu Musa, K. 22
Abu-Lughod, L. 41
Abul-Omrein, K. 18
ACNielsen 76
activism 8
agency 47–8
Ahearn, L. 48
Ahmad, S. 40
Al Huda 40
al-Rissala 21
Amin, S.N. 88
Anderson, B. 39
Arabic calligraphy 97–9
Arafat, Y. 8
architecture: mosque 94–6
army: Pakistan 59
art forms 93–104; beautiful women 103–4; mother 102; young boy 102–3
Asad, T. 47, 75, 76
Ayat-Ayat Cinta 84
Azim, F. 1–5, 87–90
Azim, S. 93–104

Banerjee, S. 60
Bangladesh 2–5, 87–90, 93–104; class 58, 88; emerged 3, 87; middle-class 58; music 58–60; nationalism 57; politics 2–3; post-liberation 61
Bano, W.S. De 64
Bardaweel, S. 22–3
Begum, A. 51
Bengali culture 3, 4
Bengali identity 62
Bengali Muslim women 3, 59–60, 87–90
boy: as art form 102–3
British India 38

calligraphy: Arabic 97–9
charitable societies 10
cinema: Indonesia 84
citizenship 25, 46–7
class: Bangladesh 58, 88; middle 58
Cohen, A. 17
colonialism 2
Complex Terrains: Islam, culture and women in Asia 1

Deeb, L. 68
democracy 24
Derrida, J. 84
Dhanraj, D.: Lalita, K. and Rajan, D. 4, 45–54
dignity 47
disasters: natural (Indonesia) 74
discourse 24–8; development 46; Islamic 25; religious 24
dress 3, 11

education 16
employment 90
empowerment 90
ensoulment 76

family 23; law 14–15
Fateh 19
feminism 8, 34–5; Pakistan 36
Festival of the Muslim Woman 10
friendship 50
fundamentalism 8

gender ideology: Hamas 7, 11, 15–17
gendered structure: Hamas 9–11
God: punishments to sinners 77–9; rewards 79–80
Grewal, I. 34
Gujarat 45; government 45, 53
Gujarat violence (2002) women's experiences 45–54; acknowledgement 53; depositions 53; friendship 50; going out 49; justice 52–4; married woman's excerpt 51; narratives 46, 48–54; police 49, 54; post-violence situation 49; POTA 53; riots 48; rupture 48; social activist's excerpt 52–3; stress 48; targeted violence 49; widow's excerpt 51

Hadith 76
Hajj 63–4
Hamas 4, 7–28; formation 8; gender ideology 7, 11, 15–17; gendered structure 9–11; leadership 14, 27; men's dominance 23; strategy change 20
Hamas Charter 19
Hammami, R. 16, 17
Haroun, A. 12, 22, 25
Hawley, J.S. 7
Hefner, R.W. 74
Hidayah (God's Guidance) 73, 77
Hindus 88–9
Hirschkind, C.: and Mahmood, S. 68
Hobsbawm, E. 8
Hossain, R.S. 88
Hunter, W.W. 88
Huq, M. 69, 88
Huq, S. 4, 57–70
husband: transformation 68

identity: Bengali 62; and representation 33–41
India 46; British 38; Muslim community 46, 51–2
India-Pakistan partition (1947) 87
Indian Musulmans, The (Hunter) 88
Indonesia 4, 73, 74; cinema 84; media 73; natural disasters 74; revival 74
Indonesian religious television series 73–85; celebrity preacher 80; contestation of Islamic teachings 80–1; critics 82; emotions 77–8; God's punishment to sinner 77–9; God's rewards 79–80; Islamic preacher 79, 82–3; moral values 81–2; music 77–8; real-life situation 80; transgendered people 81; veiled character 81–2; women stereotypes 79
Inter-Asia Cultural Studies 1
International Women's Day 10
Invisible Histories, Disappearing Women (Sarkar) 88–9
Islam 1–3, 7–8, 75
Islamic life 39
Islamic movements 16; Palestine student 10
Islamic National Salvation Party 7–9, 11–12; Consultative Council 12; General Conference 12; kindergartens 13, 15; members 12; WAD *see* Women's Action Department (WAD)
Islamic piety 73, 75–6, 83–5
Islamic Women's Movement in Palestine 14
Israeli Intelligence Service 18

Jad, I. 4, 7–28
Jahan, R. 61
Jamaat-e-Islami 33–41, 61; interlocutors 36–8
Jamaat-e-Islami women leaders 37–41; backgrounds 37–8; English language 37–8; Urdu language 37–8; Women's Commission 34; Women's Wing 33
Jama'atul Mujahideen Bangladesh (JMB) 61
Jamal, A. 4, 33–41
justice 52–4

Kandiyoti, D. 16
Keddie, N.R. 9, 16, 19
Khalil, N. 21–2, 24
Kiamat Sudah Dekat (The End is Nigh) 81–3, 84
killing: of loose women 19
kindergartens 13, 15

Lalita, K.: Rajan, D. and Dhanraj, D. 4, 45–54
law: family 14–15; penal 14–15
leaders: Hamas 14,27; Jamaat-e-Islami women 33, 34, 37–41
life phases 64
living conditions: Palestine 18–19
loose women: killing 19

Maha Kasih (The Most Gracious) 79
Mahmood, S. 47–8, 61; and Hirschkind, C. 68
marriage 66–7; arrangements 23
married woman: and Gujarat violence 51
Maududi, A.A. 33, 38–9
media: Indonesia 73
Middle East 41; society 41
middle-class: Bangladesh 58
Minority Women Negotiating Citizenship 45
Mizwar, D. 81, 83
modernism 11, 38
modesty 65–8
Mohanty, C.T. 17
Molyneux, M. 28
moral values 81–2
mosque architecture 94–6; dome 95; minaret 95; windows 94
mother: as art form 102
Muhammad, Prophet 2
Murshid, G. 59
Musharraf, P. 36
music: Bangladesh 58–60; Indonesian 77–8
music (giving up) and piety 57–70; conversation 57; Hajj 63–4; husband's transformation 68; inner self 62–5, 69; life phases 64; marriage 66–7; modesty 65–8; musical guru 63; praise 65; psychological peace 65–6; reflecting 65; religious injunctions 62; religious songs 58; role as

preacher 68; sexual potential 63; singing tutor 58; struggle 69; trophy wives 67
Muslim Brothers 10, 18
Muslim League 2
Muslim societies 2

nationalism: Bangladesh 57
Nazrul Islam, K. 58–9
negotiation 1, 3
New Media in the Muslim World (Huq) 88
non-government organisations (NGOs) 27, 90

O'Connell, J.T. 60
organisations: NGOs 27, 90; women 10
orientalism 41

Pakistan 3, 4, 33, 35–6, 39–40; army 59; feminism 36; government 36
Pakistan-India partition (1947) 87
Palestine 4, 9; charitable societies 10; conferences 220; Islamic student movement 10; living conditions 18–19; political prisoners 13, 18; universities 9–10; women's groups 14, 21; youth 9
Palestinian Authority 13
Palestinian Woman ... Where Next? (ISP Women's Dept) 20–1
peace: psychological 65–6
penal law 14–15
piety: and giving up music 57–70; Islamic 73, 75–6, 83–5; popular culture 75–6, 85
police 49, 54
political prisoners: Palestine 13, 18
politics: Bangladesh 2–3
popular piety culture 75–6, 85; visibility 75
praise 65
preachers 79, 80, 82–3
Prevention of Terrorism Act (POTA) 53
private sphere 23
psychological peace 65–6
public space 4
public sphere 23
punishment: God's 77–9

Qur'an 76

Rahasia Ilahi (God's Secret) 76, 77
Rahman, T. 37
Rajan, D.: Dhanraj, D. and Lalita, K. 4, 45–54
reflecting 65
reflexivity 34, 39–40
religious discourse 24
religious television series: Indonesian 73–85
Reshaping the Holy (Shehabuddin) 89–90
rewards: God's 79–80
rights: women 2, 20, 24, 25
riots 48

Said, E. 41
Salvation Party *see* Islamic National Salvation Party
Sarkar, M. 88–9
Schiff, Z.: and Ya'ari, E. 18
secularism 8, 27, 60
segregation 22
self: inner 62–5, 69
shari'a 14–15, 22, 27
Shehabuddin, E. 40, 89–90
El-Sheikh, N. 19
Shin Bet 18
singing tutor 58
social activist: and Gujarat violence 52–3
social life 22
South Asia 38–9, 51, 87; cultural practices 51
status: special 2
stereotypes: women 79
stress 48
Subijanto, R. 4, 73–85
Sudiro, T. 83
Suharto 74
sustainable development 20

Tagore, R. 58–9
Taraki, L. 16
television series: Indonesian religious 73–85
terror: war on 35
Torab, A. 64
transgendered people 81
trophy wives 67

universities: Palestine 9–10

values: moral 81–2
veiled character 81–2
veiling 19
violence: Gujarat *see* Gujarat violence (2002) women's experiences

war on terror 35
Warner, M. 76, 83, 84–5
West 35–6
White, J. 11
widow: and Gujarat violence 51
wives: trophy 667
women 9, 87–8; ideal 7
Women Negotiating Islam conference 1
Women's Action Department (WAD) 8, 11–15, 20–8; booklet 20–1; conferences 14, 24–5; equal pay 26; head 12; recommendations 23; segregation 22; social life 22

World of Muslim Women in Colonial Bengal, The (Amin) 88

Ya'ari, E.: and Schiff, Z. 18
Yassine, A. 14
youth: Palestine 9
Yudhoyono, S.B. 84–5
Yurchak, A. 47
Al-Zahar, M. 14, 23, 26

Printed in Canada

PGCA2024